What leaders in their fields say about this book . . .

What is more frustrating than not being able to tell others what we think? Leaders have the vocabulary power to put their thoughts in the minds of others—clearly and with impact.

> — **William W. Adams, Chairman of the Board and President, World Armstrong Industries, Inc.**

WORD POWER: Vocabulary for Success provides a practical road map to increasing one's vocabulary and should be of great assistance to anyone seeking to enhance their communication skills.

> — **Edward J. Dauber, former Assistant Attorney General of New Jersey**

Words, not bulldozers, brought down the Berlin Wall. Words have the power to make people free, to help them question the world as it is, and make a difference. That's what *WORD POWER: Vocabulary for Success* is all about.

> — **James Florio, Governor of New Jersey**

I found *WORD POWER: Vocabulary for Success* provocative and innovative. It definitely fills a niche in the thoughtful oral communication of ideas.

> — **Joseph T. Haffey, Executive Vice President (Ret.), The CIT Group**

When communication is effective, it serves as a bridge over waters that roil with confusion, doubt and ignorance. If our leaders are to continue to bring together people, governments and nations, they can turn to *WORD POWER: Vocabulary for Success* for inspiration and guidance.

> — **Daniel K. Inouye, United States Senator, Hawaii**

The reader will find *WORD POWER: Vocabulary for Success* useful in developing a more powerful vocabulary. It is written in a style that educates and entertains at the same time.

> — **Harry P. Kamen, Chairman of the Board and Chief Executive Officer, Metropolitan Life Insurance Company**

This unique book, *WORD POWER: Vocabulary for Success,* addresses the subject of verbal power in a remarkable fashion. I know readers will find it most interesting.

> — **Donald R. Keough, President and Chief Operating Officer (Ret.), The Coca Cola Company**

WORD POWER: Vocabulary for Success is a means for sharing intellectual resources, which is always in short supply.

> — **William C. Norris, Founder and Chairman Emeritus, Control Data Corporation**

Words change the world and Charles Ickowicz's book provides us with a sampling of words used by those who are considered to be "world changers".

> — **Ann W. Richards, Governor of Texas**

I believe this book represents an intelligent approach to enhance many career opportunities by providing people with a more powerful command of the language. *WORD POWER: Vocabulary for Success* is aimed at people from all walks of life but it will prove to be particularly valuable to managers and professionals in industry and government.

> — **Otavio Sinto, President, Liquid Carbonic US Industrial Gases**

Building a powerful conversational vocabulary is a must for every aspiring leader. *WORD POWER: Vocabulary for Success* is an effective and manageable guide to this important aspect of self-development.

> — **Raymond W. Smith, Chairman of the Board and Chief Executive Officer, Bell Atlantic Corporation**

I found this book to be a comprehensive and innovative approach to building a strong and distinctive vocabulary. Communication is the key to progress in our global society, and those who can articulate their thoughts and visions will be the leaders of tomorrow. This book will be an invaluable tool in the realm of communications.

> — **Robert G. Torricelli, United States Congressman, New Jersey**

To make an impact in today's fast paced world, you must be able to communicate clearly, succinctly, and in terms utilized by the pace setters. Charles Ickowicz's book provides an easy and effective way to develop language skills necessary for personal development and good communication.

> — **David W. Troast, Group Vice President, BOC Group and President, Airco Industrial Gases (Ret.)**

We are responsible for not only what we may say but also how we say it. I truly believe that this kind of book will be immensely helpful for business and government leaders, as well as for the general public.

> — **David S. Weil, President, Ampacet Corporation**

Word power:

vocabulary for success

by Charles Ickowicz

The author gratefully acknowledges permission from the following to reprint material:

ABC News, for material in *This Week with David Brinkley*.

CBS News, for material in *Face The Nation*.

The Conference Board, for material in *Across The Board*.

Discover Publications, for material in "Neatness Doesn't Count After All" by Hugh Kenner in *Discover* (1986).

Harvard University, for material in *Harvard Business Review*.

The Johnson O'Connor Research Foundation, for material in "The Vocabulary Scores of Company Presidents" by Richard M. Smith, Ph.D., and Gary P. Supanish.

NBC News, for material in *Meet The Press*.

The New York Times Company, for material in *The New York Times*.

Dashir, Inc., 458 Reis Avenue, Teaneck, NJ 07666

Copyright © 1994 by Charles Ickowicz

Published by Dashir, Inc.

Library of Congress Catalog Card Number 94–071071

ISBN 0–9635623–1–2

Printed in the U.S.A.

To my wife, Helen,
and in memory of my parents,
Louis and Janet

ACKNOWLEDGMENTS

I would like to thank the many senators, congressmen and CEOs who took time out of their very busy schedules to participate in the vocabulary test used in this book. I would also like to thank the students at the Columbia University Graduate School of Business, Dartmouth College Amos Tuck School of Business Administration, and Stanford University Graduate School of Business, who also participated in the survey. I would like to extend a special thanks to Lynn Russell, Director of the Professional Development Center, Columbia University Graduate School of Business; Mary Munter, Adjunct Professor of Management Communications, Dartmouth College Amos Tuck School of Business Administration; and Joyce Pharriss, Director of the Management Communications Skills Program, Stanford University Graduate School of Business, for so kindly distributing and administering the vocabulary test to their students.

To my editor, Robert Cohen, a special thanks for his editorial expertise and advice. My appreciation also goes to Olga Chousa for her excellent concept for the book's cover. My special thanks to Sharon Solomon for bringing this book to completion through her excellent word processing skills. Finally, to the most tireless, patient and good natured friend and typist I could ever hope for, Jeanne McAuliffe—thanks ever so much.

Table of Contents

I   Introduction

Language most shows a man; speak, that I may see thee!
— Ben Jonson

Do you speak with a broad, enriched vocabulary or a limited, impoverished vocabulary?

When you speak do your colleagues have the impression that you are an intelligent, educated, articulate individual?

Is your vocabulary enhancing or impairing opportunities for success in your career?

Would you like to talk like a leader?

Tests have shown that an enriched vocabulary—one that is responsive to all situations and representative of you as an articulate, intelligent person—is a good indicator of future success. Words are building blocks—and having the ability to use a varied and sophisticated selection of words can help build a better future for you. It can assist you by enhancing your career outlook, and consequently, your earning power.

Nearly all of the more than 400 company presidents who took part in a survey by the Johnson O'Connor Foundation agreed that building a good vocabulary was important for anyone seeking to advance in the business world.

If you agree, you're ready for the next step: building a richer, more effective vocabulary. But with more than 600,000 words in the English language, where do you begin?

Perhaps the best way to begin is at the top—listening to people who are known to have educated vocabularies. Leaders, as has been shown in many studies, are likely to use more effective, more enriched words. The highest-achieving business and government leaders of our society are executives of major corporations and United States senators and congressmen. By listening to them we will discover an ideal source of words that are sophisticated and effective.

In this book, we've done a lot of the work for you. We've examined hundreds of television, newspaper and magazine interviews with the most successful business and government leaders of our society: senators, congressmen, and chief executive officers (CEOs) from Fortune 500 companies. The firms include IBM, Xerox, General Motors, Ford, Chrysler, Exxon, Mobil, Union Carbide, and Proctor & Gamble, and financial institutions such as Citicorp, Chase Manhattan Bank, Chemical Bank, Merrill Lynch, Shearson Lehman, American Express, and Salomon Brothers.

The interview topics cover a vast spectrum, including business and economics, politics, art, education, personal goals and achievements, and family life. The interviews represent a natural choice and usage of words (as opposed to prepared speeches, which were avoided). Here we see leaders thinking on their feet and using the words they're most comfortable with—words that communicate their thoughts clearly, dynamically, succinctly.

Sample sentences in the following pages will include many actual quotes from business and government leaders.

The book also includes:

- A vocabulary test. This unique test is the only one available that compares your conversational skills to the verbal skills of 120 CEOs, senators, and congressmen. One hundred twelve MBA students at three of America's most prestigious universities have already taken the test, and their scores are provided. The test is also the first readily available measure of *conversational* vocabulary skills—as opposed to reading vocabulary comprehension. (Virtually all vocabulary tests measure reading comprehension—not necessarily a good indicator of an enriched spoken vocabulary.)

- A brief history of English. To understand words more fully, it is helpful to take a look at the roots of the language. Knowing the origins of words can serve as a memory-jogger. You will discover, for example, that *disparage* is derived from the Middle French *desparagier* meaning "to marry below one's class," and *cynic* comes from the Greek *kynikos* meaning "like a dog."

- A writer's reference guide. This reference, which is in alphabetical order by the lower level word, enables you quickly to find the higher level word for which you are looking.

If you follow the instructions in this book, you will have a feeling of accomplishment when you're finished. You will display a fuller, more varied command of language. Your verbal skills will assist in enhancing your career. You will be expressing yourself with the words leaders use—a vocabulary for success!

II The Conversational Vocabulary Test

What are the words that you use in your daily contact with the world? This test will give you a highly accurate picture of your verbal skills, as opposed to your reading comprehension.

Developed in a survey of 120 CEOs, senators, and congressmen, the test consists of 50 randomly selected words that are representative of a strong vocabulary. The test will provide a true reflection of how well you command the English language in social and business situations.

The test emphasizes two components of our vocabulary:

1. Whether we use synonyms that are enriched or simple.
2. How frequently we use these terms.

Measuring the frequency of use is important. For example, if two persons are in a situation in which they can select the word *tolerate* or the phrase *put up with* 20 times in one week, and the first person selects *tolerate* 10 times while the second uses it only once, then the first person has a more enriched vocabulary.

Following the test, you will have the opportunity to compare your scores against the scores of business and government leaders, as well as the 112 MBA students who took the test from the Columbia University Graduate School of Business, Dartmouth College Amos Tuck School of Business Administration and Stanford University Graduate School of Business.

The sentences below contain a lower-level, more simple word (a) and a higher-level, enriched word (b) that have similar meanings. Read each sentence, and ask yourself how often you would use the higher-level word in the same situation. For example, if you had the opportunity to use the words *adhere* or *stick to* in conversation 20 times in a month, how often would you say *adhere*? If your answer is occasionally, then you receive five points and you should write the number 5 in the blank following the sentence. Use your intuition, and try not to spend more than a few seconds on each example.

Frequency of Using Enriched (Italicized) Words

Frequency	Guideline	Points
frequently	at least 10 out of 20 times	10
occasionally	5 out of 20 times	5
rarely	1 out of 20 times	1
never	0 out of 20 times	0

Example:

I think the XYZ Company will (a) stick (b) *adhere* to our sales agreement. _____5_____

1. If Sue (a) reaches (b) *achieves* her goal, her salary should be increased. _____

2. Let's (a) get rid of (b) *eliminate* that product from our line. _____

3. The (a) question (b) *issue* of a more aggressive pricing policy has to be discussed. _____

4. You (a) chose (b) *selected* the best candidate for the job. _____

5. We (a) spotted (b) *identified* four areas in which we could outperform the competition. _____

6. He has (a) shown (b) *demonstrated* that he can do the job. _____

7. Miss Albert did a (a) complete (b) *comprehensive* market study. _____

8. A good system to (a) keep track of (b) *monitor* costs is vital. _____

9. We won't be able to (a) keep (b) *retain* control of the firm.

    _____

10. Will you (a) look into (b) *investigate* the question of our lower market share?

    _____

11. We should (a) buy (b) *purchase* this building.

    _____

12. (a) Leave out (b) *Omit* the comment about excessive costs from this report.

    _____

13. Were you able to (a) get (b) *obtain* the information?

    _____

14. There is no way to (a) check (b) *verify* the information so soon.

    _____

15. If Fred (a) stands in the way (b) *interferes*, we should reconsider our position on the project.

    _____

16. Market pricing looks like it will (a) get worse (b) *deteriorate*.

    _____

17. You need to (a) put together (b) *integrate* the different parts of the report.

    _____

18. Their (a) huge (b) *enormous* debt will cause problems if interest rates rise.

    _____

19. Have you (a) changed (b) *modified* your views on him since that presentation?

    _____

20. (a) Bad (b) *Adverse* economic times are causing bankruptcies.

    _____

21. My husband (a) gave up (b) *sacrificed* his career so I could advance.

    _____

22. We need to (a) speed up (b) *accelerate* the research project.

    _____

23. We have a (a) basic (b) *fundamental* conflict of interest.

    _____

24. We must be able to (a) speak to (b) *address* our clients' concerns.

    _____

25. In (a) looking back (b) *retrospect*, I see that I should have been more compromising on those issues.

    _____

26. We can (a) meet (b) *comply with* those requirements by Friday. _____

27. The company (a) came out of (b) *emerged from* bankruptcy much stronger. _____

28. We have had no (a) business deals (b) *transactions* with them this year. _____

29. (a) Copying (b) *Duplicating* their strategy won't get us ahead. _____

30. As soon as Ms. Smith retires, the company will (a) go back (b) *revert* to its old ways. _____

31. This new data base (a) eases (b) *facilitates* identifying new acquisition candidates. _____

32. His statement about the company's problems was (a) unclear (b) *ambiguous*. _____

33. You will (a) risk (b) *jeopardize* your future here with that attitude. _____

34. Please (a) put together (b) *compile* the data for the meeting. _____

35. They formed a (a) group (b) *coalition* to fight higher utility rates. _____

36. Rumors of more layoffs are causing a lot of (a) hassle (b) *turmoil* in the plant. _____

37. Susan won't (a) give up (b) *relinquish* control until she retires. _____

38. We are (a) thinking of (b) *contemplating* adding staff. _____

39. Don't (a) get involved (b) *intervene* unless you have to. _____

40. If my boss (a) wins (b) *prevails* in his fight for a larger bonus, we all win. _____

41. Ms. Jones seemed (a) worried (b) *apprehensive* about our decision. _____

42. Higher costs will definitely (a) lessen (b) *diminish* our competitiveness.   _____

43. I couldn't (a) find out (b) *ascertain* the assumptions behind his estimate, because they were proprietary.   _____

44. The high debt creates a very (a) risky (b) *precarious* situation.   _____

45. Our business will continue to (a) get smaller (b) *contract* as long as Smith & Co. competes with us.   _____

46. We signed a very (a) profitable (b) *lucrative* contract.   _____

47. The equipment always seems to (a) work improperly (b) *malfunction* in the summer.   _____

48. The new information (a) ruins (b) *invalidates* our whole strategy.   _____

49. Smith's drunken behavior was (a) shameful (b) *deplorable.*   _____

50. The rumor of a takeover (a) caused (b) *precipitated* a rapid rise in the stock price.   _____

Score

Simply add up your points for your total score.

What does your score mean? Let's compare it to those of the business and government leaders and MBA students who took this test.

	Score
50 answers of *frequently*	500
Leader – average score	**290**
50 answers which on average are *occasionally*	250
MBA students – average score	**215**
50 answers which on average are *rarely*	50
50 answers of *never*	0

If you scored 290 or greater, then you are a very strong communicator. While you may not need this book to enhance your vocabulary, you'll find it an interesting and convenient means to continue to expand your conversational vocabulary.

If your score is between 215 and 290, you can be confident that your vocabulary is working for you in enhancing your image and your career. You have good communication skills. But don't put the book down yet—there is still room for improvement.

If your score is below 215, you may wish to develop your conversational vocabulary in order to enhance your image and career outlook. You will be competing with many individuals who communicate at a higher level than you. This book will help you to speak at a more balanced level. You will soon be speaking like a leader, and it will not be long before your friends and business associates notice the difference.

III   English—Yesterday & Today

History

The English language is one of the richest in the world. Exploring its roots will help you understand and develop your vocabulary.

The history of English is the history of invasions and conquests—of languages introduced and imposed by invaders and gradually absorbed into an ever-changing tongue.

English evolved from an Indo-European language spoken by the people who inhabited an area near the Baltic Sea 5,000 years ago. Some of the people from this region migrated east into India. The ancient language of Sanskrit emerged from these people. Others went west into Europe and divided into three groups that spoke Germanic, Greek, and Latin. The Germanic branch developed the northern European languages, which include German, Dutch, English, and Swedish. The second group, who inhabited ancient Greece, developed the Greek language. Latin ultimately evolved into the southern European languages of Italian, French, and Spanish.

To show how similar these languages are, note the examples below:

Sanskrit	Greek	Latin	French	German	English
bhratar	phrater	frater	frère	bruder	brother
dvau	duo	duo	deux	zwei	two
trayah	treis	tres	trois	drei	three

The history of English can be divided into three periods:

Old English	500–1100 AD
Middle English	1100–1500 AD
Modern English	1500-Present

Old English. Its origins date from the 5th century, when Teutonic tribes from Denmark and Germany invaded England. The name *England* means "Land of the Angles," which was one of the tribes. (The others were the Saxons, Jutes, and Frisians.) Old English, also called Anglo-Saxon, was the Germanic language of these invaders. (Although the Celts, Gauls, and Romans invaded and occupied Britain prior to the Teutonic invasion, they had little impact on the development of the language. Only traces of the language of the Celts and Gauls survive in Irish and Scotch Gaelic.)

In the 6th and 7th centuries, the spread of Christianity introduced Latin and religious words into the Old English language. Such words include angel, martyr, abbot, and presbytr (priest). By the year 700, the language was known as Englisc.

In the late 700s, Britain suffered sporadic attacks from Viking invaders from Sweden and Norway. The attacks culminated in the Great Viking Invasion of 865, in which more than 200 Viking ships landed on the British coast and captured half of the country. The Vikings intermarried and integrated into British society, resulting in thousands of new words. Many of the words derived from Scandinavian have a hard *k* (skin, skill, cut) and hard *g* (get, give, egg) sound.

Middle English. The Norman invasion of England by William the Conqueror in 1066 marks the beginning of Middle English, which resulted from the infusion of French words into the language. For about 300 years, French was the official language of Britain and the language spoken by the British upper class. The majority of Englishmen, however, continued to speak English, which they augmented with many borrowed French words.

Modern English. The year 1500 was the dawn of modern English. Several factors were prominent in this evolution—the invention of the printing press, the Renaissance, and expanding exploration and trade.

The invention of the printing press in 1476 helped to crystallize the language. The publishing of books contributed to more homogeneity in English and had a stabilizing effect on the language. English was further enriched during the Renaissance, which spurred interest in the classics and resulted in the absorption of Latin and Greek words into the language.

By the end of the 16th century, thousands of words from many different languages were being added to the English language as the result of exploration and trade. According to Lincoln Barnett's *The Treasure of Our Tongue* such words include banana, cocoa, mosquito (Spanish), balcony and violin (Italian), and mustache and volunteer (French). Additional changes in the language include the greater use of *s* to signify plural (rather than *en* as in children, oxen), and the substitution of you, your, and yours for thou, thee, thy, and thine.

To learn more about this fascinating subject, one can read *The Treasure of our Tongue* by Lincoln Barnett and *The Story of English* by Robert McCrum, William Cran, and Robert MacNeil.

English Today

The English language has the largest vocabulary of any language in the world. However, only 40 percent of its words are rooted in Anglo-Saxon (Old English). The rest are derived from French, Latin, and Greek, with some contributions from virtually every other language.

Anglo-Saxon contributed many of the words we use most frequently such as *a, in, to, for, and, good, bad, come,* and *go.* In addition, of course, Anglo-Saxon provides a full spectrum of words required for normal conversation. Many of these words, however, are somewhat simpler than their counterparts derived from French, Latin, and Greek.

To prove the point, if we compare the first ten words of the book's vocabulary list, we will observe that the more sophisticated words are almost all derived from French, Latin, or Greek, whereas the simpler synonyms are mostly derived from Anglo-Saxon (Old English) or Middle English.

More Sophisticated		Less Sophisticated	
1. aberration	Latin	unusual	Latin
2. abundance	Latin	a lot	Old English
3. accelerate	Latin	speed up	Old English
4. acknowledge	Old English	admit	Latin
5. acquiesce	Latin	give in	Middle English
6. activate	Latin	start	Middle English
7. address	Latin	speak to	Old English
8. adhere	Latin	stick	Old English
9. adversarial	Latin	opposing	Latin
10. adversity	Latin	difficulty	Latin

With such a rich selection of words to choose from, it is unfortunate that many of us tend to use the same words—usually simple Anglo-Saxon words—in our conversation. Should you eliminate simple Anglo-Saxon words from your speech? By no means. You should continue to use these words, as leaders do, in order to communicate. Do, however, follow the example of business and government leaders, who enhance their conversations by selecting from the full spectrum of the English language. Your conversational skills will be greatly enriched if you begin to focus on the 60 percent of your vocabulary that you may have been neglecting—the French–, Latin–, and Greek-based expressions.

IV   Comprehension vs. Usage

Our comprehension of vocabulary words is generally much more developed than our use of these words. As typical Americans, we read and comprehend books, magazines, and newspapers written at an eighth-grade level. Unfortunately, the average spoken vocabulary tends to be much less sophisticated.

Compare the text of four "man-in-the-street" interviews that appeared in *USA Today* with an editorial in *The New York Times*. The issue addressed is nuclear power as a source of energy. In the *USA Today* interviews, the respondents are replying to the question "Should the USA build more nuclear power plants?"

Interviews from *USA Today*

"Yes, because I'd like to see us use energy other than oil. But the plants should be *monitored* more closely. Nuclear power has its advantages—it has reduced the tax rate in our state. And I think our technology is more up-to-date than some of the other power plants operating around the world."

"If they can guarantee some degree of safety to *residents* in and around a nuclear power plant, then I don't see a problem going that route. In light of the Persian Gulf situation and oil reserves that won't be around forever, we should at least rethink our position on nuclear power."

"As long as the plants are well managed and safely developed, nuclear power is a *viable* means of energy. With the recent developments in the Middle East, and the fact that so much of the world's oil supply is *generated* from Iraq and Kuwait, we don't want to rely on just one means of energy."

"No, because I don't think human beings can make them safe. I don't believe we should count on oil as a source of energy, but nuclear power scares me, and I can't stand the thought of nuclear waste. Where do we put it? I would just like to see more safe *alternatives*."

Editorial from the *New York Times*

The need for the nuclear power *option* has been growing with every new woe that strikes fossil fuels. Coal, the chief source of electricity, will rise in cost and unacceptability as the new Clean Air Act clamps down. And the Persian Gulf crisis has *underscored* the *vulnerability* of oil supplies. Although most electric utilities have largely weaned themselves from foreign oil, some 6 percent of the electricity in this country is still *generated* by burning oil—and the amount is rising. *Judicious* use of nuclear plants could halt that trend . . .

Thus the plan *issued* last week by a committee of nuclear and utility executives is a welcome step toward keeping the nuclear option available. The plan *envisages* using new types of reactors—now being built abroad with participation by American companies—that are *evolutionary* improvements over existing light-water reactors. These are supposedly 10 times safer, but still far short of the *"inherently* safe" designs sought by nuclear critics.

Most of the steps seem reasonable and many are already under way. But the plan focuses *primarily* on *procedural* or *institutional* changes. It does not solve the more important *substantive issues* that have turned the public away from nuclear power. Until the industry shows that its plants can be operated with a near-perfect safety record, that radioactive waste can be *disposed* of and that financial risks can be brought under control, nuclear power in this country will continue to *languish.*

A comparison of the *USA Today* interviews and the *New York Times* column demonstrates that people speak and read at different levels of sophistication. With the exception of five higher-level words, most young children would have no difficulty understanding the *USA Today* interviews.

In contrast, the *New York Times* editorial contains more than three times as many higher-level words that the average child wouldn't understand. These words are not unusual. Most adults and students at the junior high school level would understand them in print. However, these words are not commonly spoken.

The average person uses between 1,000 and 1,200 workable words in his lifetime, according to Dr. Mario Pei in *The Story of Language*. Speculating on the gap between spoken language and reading comprehension, Dr. Pei says that the average person's reading comprehension may be ten times greater than his spoken vocabulary.

If we were able to use many of the words we already know in conversation, we could expand our vocabulary skills dramatically.

V Reasons for Our Limited Spoken Vocabulary

Why do we choose simple over more complex words when we speak? There is no single explanation.

Perhaps the most important contribution to an enriched spoken vocabulary comes from reading and education. Reading contributes to comprehension. As you expand your comprehension, your spoken vocabulary may also expand—but only if you are active in pursuing this goal.

Another prime factor in an enriched spoken vocabulary is the home. A child nurtured in a home where parents have a sophisticated and varied vocabulary will find it more natural to employ an expanded vocabulary when he or she grows up. On the other hand, a child growing up in a home where primarily simple spoken words are used will be prone to employing simple terms as an adult.

Two other explanations for Americans' generally limited spoken vocabulary become evident if we compare ourselves to the British. First, it is generally agreed that British television provides substantially more educational and cultural programming than its American counterpart. If we study British television, we find a high vocabulary standard, in contrast to the more common English spoken on American television, which focuses on entertainment.

Second, in England the way a person uses language reflects his or her education and class in society. Consequently, language takes on a special importance to the British. In our more egalitarian society, speech tends to be less an indicator of status, so Americans feel less impetus to upgrade their simple vocabularies.

One final explanation may be the brain's inability to retain and quickly access more complex terms. "We make over 50 percent of our normal talk recycling only about 100 words," Dr. Hugh Kenner noted in an article in *Discover*. He cites the theory of Harvard philologist George K. Kipf:

> What goes on, according to Kipf, is this: Words that say much, like *entropy* and *ecliptic*, help us be brief . . . the few who know what they mean save a lot of time. But short, common words are easier on the rest of us, though it takes a lot of such words to specify what *entropy* can sew up in three syllables.

In essence, the average person reuses a few basic expressions to communicate a multiplicity of meanings. The following sentences will illustrate how we can overuse and recycle words in conversation. The words *get* and *thing* are two good examples.

get
Did you *get* (obtain) the data?
Did you *get* (receive) the magazine?
Did you *get* (understand) what he meant?
Did you *get* (purchase) the new suit?
Did you *get* (arrive) there without any problem?

thing
I need to discuss two *things* (items) with you.
Let's clarify this *thing* (issue) before we have a problem.
We have three *things* (topics) on the agenda.

The above examples demonstrate how a simple word can convey many meanings. It is easy to become overdependent on simple words and neglect developing a more sophisticated spoken vocabulary. But unless you make the effort, you will never talk like a leader.

VI   The Hierarchy of Vocabulary Words

The English language is endowed with the largest range of synonyms in the world. Note the following examples:

A. extirpate, get rid of, eradicate

B. stubborn, refractory, obstinate

C. contemplate, cogitate, think

D. abrogate, end, terminate

As you can see, these synonyms range from very simple words to those we may not even understand. How do you choose the synonyms that will work most effectively for you?

Again, look at the speech patterns of leaders. By observing the way they talk, we can construct a hierarchy of words—identifying the least and most desirable. In the following chart, we recast the words above into a simple three-tier system.

TIER III	extirpate (L)	refractory (L)	cogitate (L)	abrogate (L)
TIER II	eradicate (L)	obstinate (L)	contemplate (L)	terminate (G)
TIER I	get rid of (ME)	stubborn (ME)	think (OE)	end (OE)

L – Latin, G – Greek, ME – Middle English, OE – Old English

Tier I represents the level at which most of us speak, using simple words, which are mostly Anglo-Saxon based.

Tier II encompasses words that are commonly used in the media and by leaders. Many of these expressions are derived from French, Latin, and Greek.

Tier III words are unusual words that are seldom used in ordinary conversations. They are more likely to be used in scholarly books and journals. Generally non-Anglo-Saxon based, these are words that would often sound pretentious in conversation and impair rather than enhance oral communication.

By listening to leaders we can see that they balance their vocabularies by using both Anglo-Saxon (Tier I) and French–, Latin–, and Greek-based terms (Tier II), but they do not normally use words that are too difficult to comprehend (Tier III).

VII   Vocabulary Word List

This section will help you learn to use the words that leaders use in your day-to-day conversations. To follow are more than 335 vocabulary words followed by their roots and definitions, related words, and sample sentences.

- After each word we provide the original root of the word and its meaning, which will help you remember the word and discover interesting relationships with other words. Prefixes of roots that are used repetitively, such as *trans* (transaction, transcend), are only given the first time they are used. The historical derivation for each word is given using the following abbreviations:

AF	Anglo-French
F	French
fr.	from
G	Greek
Gmc	Germanic
I	Italian
ISV	International Scientific Vocabulary
L	Latin
L-F	Latin root that evolved into French and then was absorbed into English
MF	Middle French
OE	Old English
OF	Old French

- This book is not a dictionary. It only defines terms by their synonyms. Although many of the words have multiple meanings, in most cases only two or three common synonyms are shown.

- As you learn new expressions, you can significantly increase your vocabulary by using the word in its different forms. For each vocabulary word, related words and, in some cases, opposite words are provided to help you expand your vocabulary. For example,

tolerate	We will not *tolerate* any misbehavior during the company outing.
tolerable	Working in the factory during the summer is only *tolerable* when the air conditioning is functioning.
tolerance	The new company president has shown much *tolerance* for radical business proposals.
tolerant	The vice-president for sales has a reputation for being *tolerant* when salesmen have not met their budgets.
intolerance	*Intolerance* can be a virtue, for example, when society will not *tolerate* drinking and driving.

Many of the sample sentences provided are quotes from contemporary business and government leaders that illustrate their usage of these more enriched terms. Others are aphorisms by historical figures and were included to entertain you.

Twenty-five Vocabulary Quizzes and ten Reviews are included in this book. They will help reinforce and support your vocabulary-building program.

Now, let's get started!

- A -

aberration (*errare* to wander, err L) **something unusual, a deviation**

aberrant

The large drop in the stock market was an **aberration** in this bull market.

The sense of a company culture at Widget, Inc. is so strong that **aberrant** behavior rarely occurs.

abundance (*abundare* to abound L-F) **a lot (of), plenty (of)**

abundant
abundantly

"It should be pointed out that, in *The Detroit News*, an **abundance** of the lineage and revenue comes from the Sunday paper."
— Allen Neuharth, Chairman, Gannett Co., in *Adweek*

The right [of workers] to be full sharers in the **abundance** which is the result of their brain and brawn . . . is the glorious mission of the trade unions.
— Samuel Gompers, founder of the American Federation of Labor, 1850–1924

accelerate (*celer* swift L) **speed up, quicken**

acceleration

"Our ability to reduce cost has clearly **accelerated** over the last few years as a result of the business team approach."
— John G. Smale, Chairman and CEO, Procter & Gamble Co., in *Across the Board*

The assembly line in the factory once moved quite slowly, but lately there has been an **acceleration** in its speed.

acknowledge (*cnawen* know OE) **admit, accept; take notice of**

acknowledgment
unacknowledged (ant.)

"[The workforce's] greater reward is receiving **acknowledgment** that they did contribute to making something meaningful happen."
— Paul Cook, CEO, Raychem Corp., in *Harvard Business Review*

You will find the names of those people who helped conduct the scientific research **acknowledged** in the journal.

acquiesce (*quiescere* to be quiet L-F) **give in, agree with**
acquiescence
acquiescent

David **acquiesced** to our request for funds to modernize the company offices.

His **acquiescence** to the bank's demand for collateral made approval of the loan easy to obtain.

activate (*agere* to drive, do L-F) **start, turn on, set in motion**
activation
deactivate (ant.)
reactivate

If the new plant fails, we can **activate** the old one.

The **reactivation** of the planning committee was a surprise to everyone in the office, because it hadn't met for months.

address (*a dresser* to arrange MF) **concern oneself with; approach; speak to, talk to**

"There is a need to **address** each customer or supplier with respect to where they are in the quality process."
— Thomas F. Kennedy, President, Chemical Group, Hoechst– Celanese Corp., in *CPI Purchasing*

After several accidents on the shop floor, the plant manager finally **addressed** the problem of plant safety.

adhere (to) (*haerere* to stick L-F) **follow, support, stick (to) (colloq.)**
adherence
adherent

The principle to which our company **adheres** is: sell the best quality goods, but at a premium price.

Our **adherence** to good business practices has led to many loyal customers.

adversarial (*vertere* to turn L-F) **opposing, hostile**

adversary

"Supplier relations have to change from an **adversarial** price negotiation to a partnership that emphasizes quality, delivery and value."
> — Robert E. Flynn, Chairman and CEO, Fisher Controls International, Inc., in *CPI Purchasing*

Though they may know and like each other, two lawyers in court still battle each other as **adversaries**.

adversity (*vertere* to turn L-F) **misfortune, distress, difficulty, trouble**

adverse

Adversity reminds men of religion.
> — Livy, Roman historian, 59 B.C.–A.D. 17

The **adversity** that a company may suffer from short-term dips in business is nothing compared to the long-term trouble caused by not dealing with internal weaknesses.

advocate (*vocare* to call L-OF) **support, recommend, call for, urge**

advocacy

"John Kennedy did not sign or **advocate** the kind of tax break for the rich that is being talked about today . . . ."
> — Rep. Richard Gephardt (D–MO), on CBS News' *Face the Nation*

Despite those who doubted her view, Linda's **advocacy** of higher interest rates in order to slow down inflation was finally accepted.

aesthetic (*aistheta* things perceptible to the senses G) **dealing with the beautiful, graceful, artistic, attractive**

aesthetically

Both the content and the **aesthetic** appeal of the presentation will impress our clients.

Because we tend to prize physical attractiveness, the **aesthetic** quality of goods is often at least as important as their economic value to the customer.

- QUIZ -

Match the Tier II word in the first column with its synonym in the second column.

_____	1. abundance	a. quicken
_____	2. acquiesce	b. admit
_____	3. adversarial	c. plenty (of)
_____	4. advocate	d. trouble
_____	5. accelerate	e. dealing with beauty
_____	6. adversity	f. deviation
_____	7. activate	g. recommend
_____	8. aesthetic	h. concern oneself with
_____	9. aberration	i. stick (to)
_____	10. adhere (to)	j. opposing
_____	11. address	k. give in
_____	12. acknowledge	l. turn on

Answers:

1. c	4. g	7. l	10. i
2. k	5. a	8. e	11. h
3. j	6. d	9. f	12. b

---

affinity (*finis* end L-F) **attraction, bent**

Joe has an **affinity** for high-risk investments.

The greater the **affinity** of employees to their company, the more successful it is likely to be.

affirm (*firmare* to make firm L-F) **declare, assert, say, state**

affirmation
affirmative
reaffirm

> By investing in this plant, we're **affirming** our commitment to safety.

> More attractive to most consumers than a negative ad about its competitors is an ad that **affirms** the positive qualities of a product or service.

agenda (*agere* to drive, do L) **list of topics, list of things to be done**

> "I think we can win the White House, but we have to talk about a broader **agenda** than simply the macro issues."
> — Rep. Vin Weber (D–MN), on ABC News' *This Week with David Brinkley*

> The organized executive usually has an **agenda** in mind of the things he or she wants to do each day.

aggregate (*greg* flock L) **group; mass; total**

aggregation

> "We interrogated the President for about two and a half hours in **aggregate** in two different sessions."
> — Sen. John Tower (R–TX), on ABC News' *This Week with David Brinkley*

> Considered individually instead of in the **aggregate**, the company's problems seemed much more manageable.

alienate (*alienare* to estrange L-F) **turn off, turn against, estrange, make hostile**

alienation

> Our competition has **alienated** their customers by trying to raise prices too fast.

> By encouraging bottom-up communication, the president was able to overcome the **alienation** of workers from management.

allege (*legare* to assign L-F) **state without proof, claim, declare, charge**

allegation
allegedly

> The new secretary **alleged** that she was sexually harassed on the job; the company is now investigating her charges.

> The treasurer found it difficult to deny the **allegation** that his company had concealed losses to avoid depressing the stock price.

alleviate (*levis* light L) **relieve, lessen**

alleviation

> "I think [Gorbachev] will try to **alleviate** the effect of a strike with some kind of relief effort for consumer goods."
> — Sen. Sam Nunn (D–GA), on NBC News' *Meet The Press*

> By balancing tax increases on some items with tax credits on others, the president tried to **alleviate** the burden of the overall tax package.

altruistic (*alter* other F-L) **unselfish, devoted to others**

altruism

> "The Communications Satellite Act wasn't totally **altruistic** ... obviously the United States benefitted greatly."
> — Irving Goldstein, CEO, Comsat, in *Across the Board*

> The company donated its art collection to the museum out of **altruism**, not merely because of the tax advantages.

ambiguous (*ambi* both, around + *agere* to drive L) **unclear, vague**

ambiguity
ambiguously
unambiguous (ant.)

> In order to avoid giving away company secrets, his statements about the company's new projects were **ambiguous**.

> The uncertain future of the company caused its president to make **ambiguous** statements in the firm's annual report.

ambivalent (*valent* ISV) **of two minds, confused; mixed**

ambivalence
ambivalently
unambivalent (ant.)

> He has **ambivalent** feelings about the company relocating to Florida; the state is beautiful, but hot.

> At first she was both excited and fearful about her promotion, but Ms. Quinn's **ambivalence** soon turned to confidence as she became used to her new job.

ameliorate (*melior* better L) **make better, improve**

amelioration

> "I think understanding of both of these obstacles [American indifference and isolationism toward the contras] has been **ameliorated** due to Colonel North."
> — Rep. Henry Hyde (R–IL), on ABC News' *This Week with David Brinkley*

> Any **amelioration** of the company's financial condition depends on better defining the firm's product line.

amorphous (*morphe* form G) **shapeless, formless, vague**

amorphously

> The key ideas in the prospectus were hard to grasp because of the document's **amorphous** organization.

> The offices were designed **amorphously**; it appeared that their purposes had not been considered by the architects.

analogous (to) (*logos* reason G) **comparable, like, similar**

analogously
analogy

> "I don't want to get too much into a sports **analogy**, but if you win a game with dirty pool that doesn't advance the sport."
> — Willard C. Butcher, Chairman and CEO, Chase Manhattan Bank, N.A., in *Across the Board*

> The economy, when it's growing at record rates, is **analogous** to a ship at full throttle.

animate (*anima* breath, soul L) **give life to, make lively**

> Bob's ability to **animate** his presentation with expressions of enthusiasm and excitement won over the audience.

> Becky **animated** her talk with big gestures and humor.

anomalous (*a* without + *homos* same G) **abnormal, irregular, unusual, out of place**

anomaly

> It is **anomalous** to see someone using a slide rule in an era of calculators and personal computers.

> Lifetime employment at one company is an **anomaly** in today's rapidly changing labor market.

antagonize (*anti* against + *agon* contest G) **anger, provoke; evoke bad feeling, ill will, or hostility (in or from)**

antagonism
antagonist

> Should we **antagonize** an important customer because his payments are a few days late?

> The natural **antagonism** between competing companies does not mean they cannot cooperate in areas in which both may gain—for example, in influencing international trade policy.

- QUIZ -

Match the Tier II word in the first column with its synonym in the second column.

_____	1. agenda	a. group
_____	2. affirm	b. vague
_____	3. ameliorate	c. claim
_____	4. alleviate	d. similar
_____	5. antagonize	e. mixed
_____	6. affinity	f. assert
_____	7. analogous	g. unselfish
_____	8. ambiguous	h. list of topics
_____	9. altruistic	i. abnormal
_____	10. alienate	j. relieve
_____	11. anomalous	k. provoke
_____	12. allege	l. attraction
_____	13. ambivalent	m. make better
_____	14. aggregate	n. turn against
_____	15. amorphous	o. make lively
_____	16. animate	p. formless

Answers:

1. h	5. k	9. g	13. e
2. f	6. l	10. n	14. a
3. m	7. d	11. i	15. p
4. j	8. b	12. c	16. o

anticipate (*ante* before + *capere* to take L) **prepare for; expect, foresee**

anticipation
anticipatory

Since Sharon **anticipates** the successful introduction of three new products, her sales budget reflects 25 percent growth next year.

The big runup in the stock's price was caused by the **anticipation** of increased earnings.

antiquated (*antiquus* old L) **old, obsolete, outmoded, out-of-date**

The accounting techniques in this company are as **antiquated** as the abacus.

With its **antiquated** equipment, some of it pre-World War II, this factory is finding it difficult to compete today.

apathetic (*pathos* emotion G) **indifferent, uninterested, unconcerned**

apathy

Once Mike got the promotion, he was no longer **apathetic** about his job.

With all the exciting changes introduced by computers, it is hard to remain **apathetic** toward these amazing machines.

appease (*pax* peace L) **soothe, pacify; satisfy**

appeasement

"I think patience in the face of prolonged savagery really is not patience at all, but is a policy of **appeasement**."
— Sen. William S. Cohen (R–ME), on NBC News' *Meet The Press*

The credit department would not be **appeased** until it collected the last penny from the delinquent account.

apprehensive (*prehendere* to grasp L) **fearful, anxious, fearfully concerned, worried**

apprehension

Mike was **apprehensive** about his position in the company after it was acquired by a competitor.

Jill's **apprehension** about layoffs during the recession turned out to be unnecessary, because her company actually grew.

arbitrary (*arbiter* judge L-F) **discretionary, subjective; whimsical, random; unreasonable, dictatorial**

arbitrarily

Mr. Malachi **arbitrarily** chose June 22 for the sales meeting because every day that he suggested to the staff created a problem for someone.

Thoughtful, reasonable decisions were needed, but Ms. Jimson's decisions usually seemed **arbitrary**.

articulate [used as a verb] (*articulus* joint, division L) **say, express clearly**
   articulation

> "To lead, you've got to have a vision of the company that you are able to **articulate** and that people will believe in."
> — Geoffrey Simmonds, Chairman, Hercules Aerospace Co., in *Across the Board*

Gail's **articulation** of the company's goals was easy to understand, because she wrote clearly and concisely.

ascertain (*cernaere* to sift L-F) **determine, find out, discover**

I couldn't **ascertain** the assumptions behind his market forecast, because the statistics he used were proprietary.

Ms. Emerson closely examined the company's financial records to **ascertain** whether it would be a good investment.

aspiration (*spirare* to breathe L) **hope, desire, goal**
   aspire

> "We need to get the deficit down, but we should not try to balance the budget off the backs of poor people or their **aspirations**."
> — Jack Kemp, Secretary of Housing and Urban Development and former Congressman, on NBC News' *Meet the Press*

Not content with her low-level job in the corporation, Jane **aspired** to a higher position.

atrophy (*trephein* to nourish G) **waste away, decline**

Neglected by the rest of the firm, the research department **atrophied** and soon lost all of its old punch.

After Dana left the company, the whole back office seemed to **atrophy** from lack of purpose.

attain (*tangere* to touch L-F)   **reach, gain**
attainable
unattainable (ant.)

> Our district **attained** its sales goal in record time.

> Because he had the necessary skills and experience, Joe felt that his job goal was **attainable**.

attribute [used as a noun] (*tribuere* to bestow L)   **characteristic, quality**

> There is no greater **attribute** of the superior person than helping others to practice virtue.
> — Meng-tse, Chinese philosopher, 372–289 B.C.

> There's no question that David has the **attributes** necessary to become president of this company.

attrition (*attritio* gradual wearing down L)   **gradual wearing down; decreasing in size or number; thinning out**

> Losing employees by **attrition** takes much longer than laying them off all at once.

> We lost half of the office softball team through **attrition**; several members were transferred to another facility, and the rest left the company.

augment (*augere* to increase L-F)   **add to, increase, enlarge**
augmentation

> "It's a small staff, but it's **augmented** by volunteers in the community—executives, professional people, professors at universities, and so forth."
> — William C. Norris, Chairman, Control Data Corp., in *Across The Board*

> Wilma added several new specialists to her team; this **augmentation** enabled her to bring in more business.

auspicious (*auspex* diviner by birds L, fr. *avis* bird + *specere* to look)   **favorable, promising, timely**
inauspicious (ant.)

> With the Dow-Jones index rising so fast, this could be an **auspicious** time to invest.

Although she later became division chief, her arrival was relatively **inauspicious**—few people even bothered to say hello.

authorize (*augere* to increase L-F) **allow, permit, entitle**
authoritative
authority
authorization

The company president **authorized** me to spend up to $1 million on new computers.

Because of her considerable experience with planning, her views on the subject were considered quite **authoritative**.

- QUIZ -

Match the Tier II word in the first column with its synonym in the second column.

_____	1. apathetic	a. determine
_____	2. attain	b. fearful
_____	3. articulate	c. quality
_____	4. augment	d. foresee
_____	5. antiquated	e. permit
_____	6. authorize	f. subjective
_____	7. ascertain	g. add to
_____	8. apprehensive	h. reach
_____	9. auspicious	i. old
_____	10. attribute	j. desire
_____	11. anticipate	k. express
_____	12. aspiration	l. favorable
_____	13. arbitrary	m. uninterested
_____	14. atrophy	n. gradual wearing down
_____	15. attrition	o. soothe
_____	16. appease	p. waste away

Answers:

1. m	5. i	9. l	13. f
2. h	6. e	10. c	14. p
3. k	7. a	11. d	15. n
4. g	8. b	12. j	16. o

Review Letter A

Which Tier II words are most closely synonymous with the italicized words in the following list of sentences? The first letter of the synonym is shown. This hint will be more helpful when several letters are reviewed together, later in the book. In some cases, there is more than one correct answer.

PART A

1. Our policy is not to *provoke* the customer, even if he or she starts a confrontation with the clerk. a_____

2. This chart makes it easy to see what our earnings were, in *total*, for the year. a_____

3. Mary brought a *list of topics* to give focus to our staff meeting. (an) a_____

4. It was hard to quit smoking, but chewing gum made it easier for me to *stick* to my resolution. a_____

5. Leslie announced plans to *start* our city-wide charity drive in time for the holiday season. a_____

6. Mr. Boggs' multimedia show made his weekly sales presentation more *lively*. a_____

7. Although this line of electronic gadgets is new, the strategy to promote it is *similar* to past marketing plans. a_____

8. After weeks of defending the unproductive plant, Leo was forced to *give in* to the board's demand that he close it. a_____

9. Would you please *find out* the most efficient route to the Convention Center? a_____

10. Jack found it hard to *express* his joy and appreciation for winning the Oscar for Best Actor. a_____

11. I don't *expect* another day as warm as today until next summer. a_____

12. Are the plastic bottles supposed to be green, or is this batch a *deviation* from the norm? (an) a_____

13. Following this very successful year, I want to *state* my
    appreciation to the staff for their hard work.
    a_____

14. Although we were *fearful* of a takeover by a large corporation,
    the company remains in the family's hands.
    a_____

15. Janet prefers the four-color brochure, but I have more of an
    attraction to the simple black and white one.
    a_____(for)

PART B

1. Mr. Wiley told Aaron that he could go home early if two aspirin
   didn't *relieve* his discomfort. a_____

2. Rochelle's *goal* was to be a CEO by the age of 26. a_____

3. Jack had a *lot* of energy when he returned from his vacation.
   (an) a_____

4. Jody's jeans and T-shirt were *out of place* in the corporate
   environment. a_____

5. Once we saw the mid-year forecast, we were certain we could
   reach our sales projections. a_____

6. Lance insisted that he keep his manual typewriter, despite our
   protests that it was *obsolete*. a_____

7. The drop in interest rates was *favorable*, because we just
   started looking for a house to buy. a_____

8. I am confident that if I *speed up* the pace of my work, I will be
   rewarded with a raise. a_____

9. It was *unselfish* of Bert to finish my project so that I could go to
   the conference. a_____

10. Grace did not hesitate to *admit* that she had received a great
    deal of support from the rest of the basketball team.
    a_____

11. Since Beth was usually so conciliatory, we were surprised
    when she became *hostile* during the staff meeting.
    a_____

12. The direction of my career is *unclear*: I am considering job
    offers at an engineering firm and at a software
    company. a_____

13. George was nervous whenever he had to *speak to* the board of directors. a_____

14. Although Sue loves vacations, she says her mind begins to *waste away* after more than a week away from work. a_____

15. Larry, a current-events buff, did not understand how anyone could be *unconcerned* about national news. a_____

PART C

1. The mayor *recommends* a building program to ease the city's cramped office conditions. a_____

2. Do you think Dr. Smith will *permit* such a large expenditure for office supplies? a_____

3. When Jason asked whether I had declared a major, I responded that I had *mixed* feelings about the decision. a_____

4. Glen intends to *increase* the sales force with the addition of two regional representatives. a_____

5. Sales were down last month, but the coming holidays should *improve* the situation. a_____

6. Yolanda's choice of car seemed *random*. a_____

7. The baseball team was *supposedly* involved in an illegal gambling scheme. a_____

8. Lou is at his best when faced with *trouble*. a_____

9. Although my idea for a new computer game was still *vague*, the software company was confident it would sell. a_____

10. The new store's blaring music and garish colors *turned off* many customers. a_____

11. Liz has the right *characteristics* for success. a_____

12. To stand out from the competition, a product's packaging must appeal to the buyer's *artistic* sense. a_____

13. Our boss has decided to decrease the staff size through *a gradual thinning* rather than a wholesale layoff. a_____

14. We prefer to be kind to our customers from the start so that we don't have to *soothe* them later. a_____

Answers

A.
1. alienate/ antagonize
2. aggregate
3. agenda
4. adhere
5. activate
6. animated
7. analogous
8. acquiesce
9. ascertain
10. articulate
11. anticipate
12. aberration
13. affirm
14. apprehensive
15. affinity

B.
1. alleviate
2. aspiration
3. abundance
4. anomalous
5. attain
6. antiquated
7. auspicious
8. accelerate
9. altruistic
10. acknowledge
11. adversarial
12. ambiguous
13. address
14. atrophy
15. apathetic

C.
1. advocates
2. authorize
3. ambivalent
4. augment
5. ameliorate
6. arbitrary
7. allegedly
8. adversity
9. amorphous
10. antagonized/ alienated
11. attributes
12. aesthetic
13. attrition
14. appease

- B -

belligerent (*belligerare* to wage war L) **quarrelsome, combative, warlike**

belligerence
belligerently

> The Vice President of Sales is assertive but not **belligerent** under pressure.

> John was stubborn in defending his position on the buyout, but he never lost his temper or became **belligerent**.

beneficial (*bene* well + *facere* to do L) **good, rewarding, useful**

benefit

> If you feel that a communications training program would be **beneficial** for our employees, then let's institute it.

> When employees feel that what they are doing is **beneficial** to themselves, it is easier to increase their productivity.

benevolent (*bene* well + *velle* to wish L) **kind, good, giving**

benevolence
benevolently

> Man is certainly a **benevolent** animal. A never sees B in distress without thinking C ought to relieve him directly.
> — Sydney Smith, English writer, 1771–1845

> The company was highly regarded both for its **benevolence** toward its employees and for its innovation.

bizarre (*bizzare* brave, soldierly F) **crazy, fantastic, strange**

> The stock market's behavior is **bizarre**; it keeps rising despite all of the bad news.

> Whereas most companies work to present a cool, rational image to the public, Widgets, Inc. presented a **bizarre** image to create interest and high visibility.

- C -

candid (*candide* guileless F) **straightforward, frank, honest, open**
candidly
candidness

> As consultants, we must be **candid** with management about the problems we see and their possible solutions.

> Ms. Myers gained the trust and respect of her audience by speaking **candidly** of the firm's need for belt-tightening.

capitulate (*caput* head L) **give in, give up, surrender**
capitulation

> After four unsuccessful years trying to get a foothold in the U.S. market, the Korean steel company **capitulated** to the competition and left the market.

> It is a difficult task in business to keep sight of one's goals without **capitulation** on any key point.

capricious (*capro* goat I) **changeable, whimsical, unstable**
caprice
capriciously
capriciousness

> "There was no **capricious** thinking. We did an in-depth risk analysis."
> — J. Tracy O'Rourke, President and CEO, Allen-Bradley Co., in *Harvard Business Review*

> The only difference between a **caprice** and a lifelong passion is that the **caprice** lasts a little longer.
> — Oscar Wilde

chagrin (*chagrin* sad F) **distress, dismay, bother**

> Edgar was **chagrined** to realize that with a little more effort he could have doubled his commissions.

> Imagine Carol's **chagrin** when she discovered she was losing one of her company's best officers to the competition.

circumvent (*circum* around + *venire* to come L) **go around, evade, bypass**

circumvention

> "It showed the President's style of delegating . . . allowing those who **circumvent** the process to really be able to run their own operation."
> > — Sen. Nancy Kassebaum (R–KS), in *The New York Times*

> Until outside auditors discovered the scheme, Mr. Keene was able to conceal his illegal **circumvention** of the rules.

coalition (*alescere* to grow L-F) **group**

coalesce

> "This is a **coalition** of 175 different organizations— universities and businesses . . . ."
> > — William C. Norris, Chairman, Control Data Corp., in *Across the Board*

> Judy's position on discount sales was accepted when several factions in the company **coalesced** to support her point of view.

cognizant (*gnoscere* to come to know L) **aware, conscious**

cognizance

> The company is **cognizant** of the need to educate the public about its commitment to a safe environment.

> In order for the company's long-term plan to succeed, employees must have greater **cognizance** of productivity goals.

coherent (*haerere* to stick L-F) **consistent, logical, connected**

coherence
incoherence (ant.)
incoherent (ant.)

> The subject was very difficult and convoluted, but the presentation was **coherent** and easy to follow.

> After Cindy eliminated the inconsistencies and added logical connections to her presentation, the speech had much greater **coherence**.

collaborate (*laborare* to labor L) **work together, join forces, cooperate**
collaboration
collaborative

> Every year Jack and Corinna **collaborated** on a company musical, with Jack writing the words and Corinna the music.

> With each applying his or her own expertise to the problem, Will and Jane's **collaboration** resulted in an effective solution to the problem of worker absences.

compel (*pellere* to drive L-F) **make, force, require**
compulsory
compulsion

> Low market prices will **compel** us to modernize our plant.

> The committee is not sure whether to make wearing the safety gear optional or **compulsory**.

compensate (*pendere* to weigh L) **pay, pay back, repay, make up (for)**
compensation
compensatory

> If we take them to a Yankees ball game, that should **compensate** for all of their overtime.

> This job provides health benefits and overtime pay as well as the regular **compensation**.

compile (*compilare* to plunder L-F) **put together, collect, gather**
compilation

> Please **compile** the data we will need for the meeting.

> The **compilation** of data from all parts of the company will aid us in knowing more about the firm's workers.

- QUIZ -

Match the Tier II word in the first column with its synonym in the second column.

_____	1. benevolent	a. surrender
_____	2. circumvent	b. frank
_____	3. collaborate	c. force
_____	4. candid	d. aware
_____	5. compel	e. quarrelsome
_____	6. bizarre	f. work together
_____	7. coalition	g. changeable
_____	8. capitulate	h. kind
_____	9. compensate	i. bypass
_____	10. cognizant	j. dismay
_____	11. belligerent	k. gather
_____	12. compile	l. good
_____	13. capricious	m. pay back
_____	14. coherent	n. group
_____	15. beneficial	o. logical
_____	16. chagrin	p. strange

Answers:

1. h	5. c	9. m	13. g
2. i	6. p	10. d	14. o
3. f	7. n	11. e	15. l
4. b	8. a	12. k	16. j

complacent (*placere* to please L) **self-satisfied, smug, overly content**

complacency
complacently

> "I don't think the oil industry was **complacent** [because it had not had previous accidents]. I think what we had was a tragic human error that put this ship on the rocks."
> — Lawrence Rawl, Chairman, Exxon Corp., on CBS News' *Face The Nation*

Susan's easy-to-please nature may turn to **complacency** unless she develops more ambitious goals for herself.

comply (with) (*complere* to complete L) **satisfy, obey, meet**

compliance
compliant

"I believe that Senator Kennedy and Senator Metzenbaum are trying to change those statutes to **comply** with the Supreme Court's decision . . . ."
— Sen. Robert Dole (R–KS), on CBS News' *Face The Nation*

Has the company broken the law on stack emissions, or is it in **compliance** with all regulations?

comprehensive (*prehendere* to grasp L) **complete, thorough, all-inclusive**

The accounting department put together a **comprehensive** report about our payroll procedures.

Julia was hired after a **comprehensive** review of her application, including background checks, several interviews, and a meeting of the department.

conciliatory (*concilium* council L) **agreeable, obliging, friendly, peace-making**

conciliate
conciliation

Sue became very **conciliatory** following her argument over the sales budget.

The mayor **conciliated** the demands of both management and labor, eventually bringing them to an agreement.

condone (*donare* to give L) **forgive, excuse, pardon, overlook**

The company can't **condone** even small cases of padding one's expenses.

Because the employee had not been properly warned, his unprofessional behavior on the company outing was **condoned** by the company.

congenial (*gignere* to beget L)   **agreeable, friendly, pleasant**

congeniality

> The workers here have **congenial** relationships because we foster an apolitical environment.

> Although John's boss is usually **congenial**, sometimes she can be quite unfriendly.

conjecture (*jacere* to throw L)   **suspicion, conclusion from appearances, guess**

conjectural

> Since we had no way of knowing for sure who would be the next division chief, our discussion was full of **conjecture**.

> Theories about the future of the former Soviet Union are at this point **conjectural**.

constitute (*statuere* to set L)   **make up, form, compose**

constituent

> From the feelings proper to it, [a person's] nature is **constituted** for the practice of what is good.
> > — Meng-tse, Chinese philosopher, 372–289 B.C.

> In war, morale **constitutes** three-quarters, the balance of manpower counts for only one-quarter.
> > — Napoleon Bonaparte

contemplate (*templum* space for observation of auguries L)   **consider, study, think deeply about**

contemplation
contemplative

> After twenty years in a successful business career, Allen **contemplated** resigning from his position in order to study medicine.

> Several months of serious **contemplation** came before the company's announcement that it would begin an international division.

contentious (*contendere* to contend L-F) **quarrelsome, argumentative, belligerent**

contentiously
contentiousness

> Albert is one of the most **contentious** individuals I know; he always seems to be arguing over something.

> Away from work Nan and Tony are quite friendly with each other, but in company matters they bicker **contentiously**.

contrition (*terere* to rub L-F) **regret, remorse, sorrow**

contrite

> Max's genuine **contrition** over his company's release of pollutants into the air convinced the city council not to impose a fine.

> Though Barbara's accounting error cost the company a great deal, she was forgiven because of her **contrite** attitude.

controversy (*contra* against + *vertere* to turn L) **disagreement, difference of opinion, debate**

controversial

> "Today there is enormous **controversy** on the question of abortion."
> — Sen. Arlen Specter (R–PA), on ABC News' *This Week with David Brinkley*

> The company dress code was very **controversial** among the employees, many of whom thought dress a personal matter.

conversion (*vertere* to turn L-F) **switch, change, changeover, alteration**

convert

> "We make loans to increase the efficiency of the public sector and encourage the **conversion** of the public sector to private enterprise."
> — Barber B. Conable, Jr., President, World Bank and former Congressman, in *The New York Times*

> The corporation saved millions of dollars by **converting** from electric to gas heating.

conviction (*vincere* to conquer L) **view, belief, opinion, faith**

The supreme happiness of life is the **conviction** that we are loved.

— Victor Hugo, French author, 1802–1885

Because of our president's strong **convictions** on the importance of education, he instituted a program that paid bonuses to all employees for taking night school courses.

corroboration (*roborare* to strengthen F-L) **act of making more certain, act of confirming, confirmation**

corroborate

The **corroboration** of Mike's theory of how the company managed to expand so successfully must await full publication of company records.

Before announcing the results of the new drug, the scientists tried to **corroborate** their results by doing another experiment.

criterion (*kriterion* a means for judging G) **measure, standard, test**

criteria

The company was successful by the most important **criterion** one could apply to it—profitability.

Joan scored high on all the **criteria** for entry to management school: character, experience, and skills.

culpability (*culpa* guilt L-F) **guilt, blame**

culpable

" . . . this investigative process could . . . lead to a determination that there was no **culpability**."

— Sen. John Tower (R–TX), on ABC News' *This Week with David Brinkley*

Although Joe entered the insider trading scheme only to help others, from a legal point of view he was just as **culpable** of the crime.

curtailment (*curtus* shorten L) **cutback, reduction, shortening**

curtail

"There is going to be some **curtailment** in the benefits if the [tax] rates are to drop that much."
> — Sen. Lloyd Bentsen (D–TX), on CBS News' *Face The Nation*

As she grew closer to retirement, Stacey **curtailed** her hours and took longer vacations.

cynic (*kynikos* like a dog G-F) **one who believes that people are motivated solely by self interest**

cynical
cynicism

What is a **cynic**? A man who knows the price of everything, and the value of nothing.
> — Oscar Wilde

The press was **cynical** about the candidate's inflated platform.

- QUIZ -

Match the Tier II word in the first column with its definition or synonym in the second column.

_____	1. conciliatory	a.	act of confirming
_____	2. contrition	b.	argumentative
_____	3. complacent	c.	friendly
_____	4. controversy	d.	guilt
_____	5. constitute	e.	obey
_____	6. curtailment	f.	consider
_____	7. comply	g.	change
_____	8. conviction	h.	agreeable
_____	9. condone	i.	belief
_____	10. contemplate	j.	compose
_____	11. conjecture	k.	sorrow
_____	12. culpability	l.	content
_____	13. congenial	m.	cutback
_____	14. contentious	n.	thorough
_____	15. comprehensive	o.	disagreement
_____	16. conversion	p.	pardon
_____	17. cynical	q.	suspicion
_____	18. corroboration	r.	measures
_____	19. criteria	s.	believing people are selfish

Answers:

1. h	6. m	11. q	16. g
2. k	7. e	12. d	17. s
3. l	8. i	13. c	18. a
4. o	9. p	14. b	19. r
5. j	10. f	15. n	

Review Letters B-C

Write each word next to the sentence containing the italicized synonym.

PART A

1. The members of the horticulture club decided to *work together* on a community vegetable garden. c_____

2. In *considering* my career options, I realized that what I enjoy is more important than making a lot of money. c_____

3. Our boss will finally *switch* his manual filing system to the computer. c_____

4. It took 400 newspaper clippings to *put together* a chronology of the environmental legislation. c_____

5. Although Joan wouldn't *excuse* smoking, she permitted the company to have a smoking section in the cafeteria. c_____

6. I will not *give in* to the temptation to betray a confidence. c_____

7. Jim is looking for a way to *get around* the cumbersome requirements of his contract. c_____

8. No one can *force* you to do what you think is unjust. c_____

9. The subject of "the right to bear arms" will inevitably lead to a *dispute.* c_____

10. Lynn was *bothered* by her co-workers' lack of interest in helping out when there was a lot of work in the office. c_____

11. It was my *belief* that I could get my master's degree while working full-time. c_____

PART B

1. George was *frank* about our need to work overtime this month. c_____

2. Ms. Gillis is hoping that my research provides the necessary *confirmation* of her study. c_____

3. An analysis of the past season's expenses would be *useful* for planning ahead. b_____

4. Are you *aware* of the fact that if you don't start a savings plan now you probably will not have enough money for retirement? c_____

5. You never know with Henry; he often makes *whimsical* decisions. c_____

6. The sudden thunderstorm was *strange*, given the sunny forecast. b_____

7. There is much *suspicion* surrounding Dr. Kale's whereabouts. c_____

8. The board of directors abandoned its plans for a *reduction* of the advertising budget. c_____

9. The billing department began a *thorough* overhaul of its collection procedures. c_____

10. The senator's *quarrelsome* filibuster won no new voters to his side. b_____

11. The fire inspectors demanded that the school district *satisfy* a new set of safety requirements. c_____ (with)

12. The colorful murals will make our office a more *pleasant* place to work. c_____

PART C

1. Mr. Davis offered to *make up for* the time we spent attending evening meetings. c_____

2. Although Peggy disagreed with the debate team's conclusion, she had to admit its arguments were *consistent*. c_____

3. The raw materials cost *makes up* fifty percent of our production costs. c_____

4. Louis is an arrogant and *argumentative* person. c_____

5. Mrs. Kravitz is a *kind* employer. b_____

6. Quietly retreating to his office, Greg was *agreeable* after the confrontation. c_____

7. No one person is *guilty* for the fiasco. c_____

8. Jill abandoned her plans for medical school, having become *very content with* her typing job. c_____

9. Crying tears of *remorse*, Ben apologized for taking the box of pens. c_____

10. The activists formed a *group* to oppose the Supreme Court nominee. c_____

11. Never trusting anyone's motives, Jane is a *person who believes others are always acting selfishly.* c_____

12. Our new video camera meets all the *standards* for sales overseas. c_____

Answers

A.
1. collaborate
2. contemplating
3. convert
4. compile
5. condone
6. capitulate
7. circumvent
8. compel
9. controversy
10. chagrined
11. conviction

B.
1. candid
2. corroboration
3. beneficial
4. cognizant
5. capricious
6. bizarre
7. conjecture
8. curtailment
9. comprehensive
10. belligerent
11. comply
12. congenial

C.
1. compensate
2. coherent
3. constitutes
4. contentious
5. benevolent
6. conciliatory
7. culpable
8. complacent (about)
9. contrition
10. coalition
11. cynic
12. criteria

- D -

debacle (*de* from + *bacler* to bar MF) **rout, disaster, collapse, breakdown**

> The news of higher taxes and rising inflation caused a **debacle** in the stock market.

> The accusation of insider trading resulted in a **debacle** for the whole company and its president.

debilitate (*debilitare* to weaken L-F) **weaken**

debilitative
debility

> "It's **debilitating** to the organization itself when employees see fellow workers who are marginal, and they know it, and everyone else knows it."
> — John G. Smale, Chairman and CEO, Procter & Gamble Co., in *Across the Board*

> Lower-priced imports have had a **debilitative** effect on the clothing industry.

definitive (*finire* to limit L-F) **final, decisive, conclusive**

definitively

> We should get a **definitive** answer from the president by Friday.

> Having toured the entire factory, Ms. Moore could say **definitively** that there were no injuries in the plant explosion.

deleterious (*deleter* destroyer G) **harmful, bad, negative**

> "I have not changed my opinion about ever accepting a tax that will have a **deleterious** effect on the economy."
> — Ronald Reagan, on ABC News' *This Week with David Brinkley*

> The restrictions on smoking have had a **deleterious** effect on most tobacco companies.

delineation   (*linea* line L)   **description, outline; definition**
delineate

> "We need to have a clear **delineation** as to where United
> States military force is going to be used."
> — Sen. John McCain (R–AZ), on CBS News' *Face The
> Nation*

> So that the antitrust ruling would be clear, Judge Walker
> carefully **delineated** each point in her opinion.

demeanor   (*mener* to lead, drive, conduct L)   **outward manner,
bearing, deportment**

> Throughout the hearing, Barry's **demeanor** never varied from
> an appearance of calm, patient strength.

> Hildegard's smooth **demeanor** never betrayed the inner
> uncertainty she felt.

demise   (*mittere* to send L-F)   **end, death, dying**

> The company had been losing market share for so long that its
> **demise** seemed only a matter of time.

> The **demise** of the steel industry has led many of its workers
> back to school to learn new skills.

denigrate   (*nigrare* to blacken L)   **put down, belittle**
denigration

> "I have never **denigrated** a Japanese product or a citizen of
> Japan."
> — Lee Iacocca, Chairman and CEO, Chrysler Corp., on
> CBS News' *Face The Nation*

> The company's human resources guidelines make **denigration**
> of any ethnic group a cause for dismissal.

deplorable   (*plorare* to wail L-F)   **very bad; shameful; sad, pitiful;
condemnable**
deplore

> The existence of poverty in such a wealthy country is
> **deplorable**.

> We all **deplore** the increase in crime, which has made many
> people afraid to go out at night.

designate (*signare* to mark L)   **point out, set apart, select; appoint**
designation

> Men are **designated** from the moment of birth to rule or be
> ruled.
> — Aristotle

> The **designation** of Vern as liaison between the two
> departments will promote better communication.

deteriorate (*deterior* worse L)   **get worse, worsen, decline**
deterioration

> It looks like market pricing will **deteriorate** until suppliers
> stop adding more production capacity.

> The recently purchased office equipment **deteriorated** quickly
> until it was unusable.

detrimental (*terere* to rub L-F)   **harmful, damaging**
detriment

> "[President Bush] made it clear that the use of force in Eastern
> Europe by the Soviets would be a very **detrimental** thing."
> — James A. Baker III, Secretary of State, on CBS News'
> *Face The Nation*

> Far from helping those who want to come here, the new
> immigration policy may only work to their **detriment**.

- QUIZ -

Match the Tier II word in the first column with its synonym(s) in the second column.

_____	1. deleterious	a. weaken
_____	2. demeanor	b. definition
_____	3. designate	c. pitiful
_____	4. debacle	d. final
_____	5. denigrate	e. worsen
_____	6. delineation	f. end
_____	7. detrimental	g. appoint
_____	8. debilitate	h. damaging
_____	9. deplorable	i. disaster
_____	10. deteriorate	j. belittle
_____	11. definitive	k. harmful
_____	12. demise	l. outward manner

Answers:

1. h, k	4. i	7. h, k	10. e
2. l	5. j	8. a	11. d
3. g	6. b	9. c	12. f

---

dialogue (*legein* to speak G) **talk, conversation, discussion, (verbal) exchange**

> By maintaining a regular **dialogue** with each of his vice presidents, the president remained very well informed of all the company problems and opportunities.

> The once silent and suspicious neighbors are now having an open **dialogue** in order to get to know each other.

dichotomy (*dich* apart + *temnein* to cut G) **sharp division, split, schism**

> "There is a **dichotomy** between the short-term fellow, living today and trying to get as much profit as he can, and the long-term planner."
> — Rawleigh Warner Jr., CEO, Mobil Corp., in *Across the Board*

Managers must often deal with the **dichotomy** between management and labor's conflicting interests.

differentiate (*dis* apart + *ferre* to carry L-F) **make or show to be different or distinct; contrast, set off, distinguish**

differentiation
undifferentiated (ant.)

In order to be successful in this market, we need to **differentiate** our product from the competition.

Even with unit pricing, the **differentiation** between brands of paper towels, for example, can be hard to make.

digress (*gradi* to step L) **ramble, wander, get off the topic**

digression
digressive

Our meetings always seem productive, and we rarely **digress** from the agenda.

The speaker made so many **digressions** from his stated topic that it was difficult to know what his real subject was.

dilemma (*di* two + *lemma* assumption G) **difficult problem, difficult or unsatisfactory choice, fix, double bind**

"The availability of human spare parts like hearts and kidneys will create some real **dilemmas** for society."
— Walter Wriston, former Chairman, Citicorp, in *Manhattan, Inc.*

In trying to decide the exact mix of spending cuts and tax hikes, the budget planners face some cruel **dilemmas**.

dimension (*metiri* to measure L-F) **element, aspect; size**

"I think electronic mail is going to create a brand-new business **dimension** rather than replacing existing business."
— John C. Emery, Jr., CEO, Emery Air Freight Corp., in *Planning Review*

The oil spill was so enormous that the company did not know its full **dimensions** for many weeks.

diminish (*minuere* to lessen L-F) **lower, lessen, reduce, shrink**

The higher costs we've incurred will **diminish** our competitiveness.

In spite of the losses sustained in the last quarter, the company's profits for the year were not **diminished**.

disarray (*areer* to put in order OF) **mess, disorder, confusion**

"I like a business where the marketplace is in turmoil, the competition is in **disarray** and you have all the financial resources in the world and good talent."
>   — Michael Carpenter, CEO, Kidder, Peabody & Co., Inc., in *The New York Times*

Linda's office is always in such **disarray** that it is amazing she can work in that environment.

discern (*cernere* to sift L-F) **see, notice, detect**

discernible

" . . . Leadership involves **discerning** what is in the national interest, not simply listening to the loudest voices that are heard in the capital."
>   — Sen. George J. Mitchell (D–ME), on NBC News' *Meet The Press*

Amid the conflicting data about the stock, there was no **discernible** pattern that would help predict its future earnings.

discretion (*cernere* to sift L-F) **tact, prudence, good judgment**

discreet

Satire's my weapon, but I'm too **discreet**
To run amuck, and tilt at all I meet.
>   — Alexander Pope, English poet, 1688–1744

Joan has always shown great **discretion** in handling difficult business situations.

disenchantment (*enchanter* to enchant MF) **disillusionment, unhappiness**

disenchanted

"I'm finding **disenchantment** with some of the things we've done [in Congress] and I'll be responsive to that."
— Sen. Paul Laxalt (R–NV), on ABC News' *This Week with David Brinkley*

When politicians cannot deliver on their promises, voters often become **disenchanted**.

- QUIZ -

Match the Tier II word in the first column with its synonym in the second column.

_____	1. dilemma	a. split
_____	2. disarray	b. notice
_____	3. dialogue	c. ramble
_____	4. disenchantment	d. disorder
_____	5. dimension	e. distinguish
_____	6. dichotomy	f. good judgment
_____	7. diminish	g. aspect
_____	8. discretion	h. unhappiness
_____	9. differentiate	i. discussion
_____	10. discern	j. difficult choice
_____	11. digress	k. reduce

Answers:

1. j	4. h	7. k	10. b
2. d	5. g	8. f	11. c
3. i	6. a	9. e	

---

disparage (*desparagier* to marry below one's class MF) **badmouth, belittle, put down**

disparagement
disparagingly

"[Congressman] Bill [Gray] **disparages** the [economic] recovery ...."
— Rep. Jack Kemp (R–NY), on ABC News' *This Week with David Brinkley*

The praise of Stan's accomplishments was a more effective strategy than the **disparagement** of his failures.

disparity (*paritas* parity L-F) **difference, inequality**

disparate

> There is a large **disparity** in the salaries of manual laborers and their supervisors in our company.

> Because their personalities are so **disparate**, it's hard to see how the co-executives get along with each other.

disproportionate (*portio* portion L-F) **unequal, uneven, unusually large**

disproportionately

> "We are still paying a hugely **disproportionate** share of the cost of defending Europe and Asia."
> > — Sen. Albert Gore, Jr. (D–TN), on ABC News' *This Week with David Brinkley*

> A **disproportionately** large part of our budget goes to pay the national debt, leaving less and less money to provide services and promote economic growth.

disseminate (*seminare* to sow L) **spread widely, distribute**

dissemination

> It is often difficult to **disseminate** important information in a large organization.

> The firm depended on its public relations department for quick **dissemination** of the news of its victory in court.

dissipate (*supare* to throw L) **scatter, spread; waste**

dissipation

> Bob **dissipated** his inheritance in the commodity market, trying to make a quick buck.

> In eighteenth century London, historian Edward Gibbon saw only "crowds without company, and **dissipation** without pleasure."

dissuade (*suadere* to urge L-F) **turn aside, discourage**

"The fact that we'd built up our own armed forces . . . [and] sent troops to Europe—all of that I think **dissuaded** [Khrushchev]."
> — Sen. Robert F. Kennedy (D–NY), in *Robert Kennedy: In His Own Words*

Because of the large costs involved, manufacturers are often **dissuaded** from upgrading their heavy plant equipment.

divisiveness (*dis* apart + *videre* to separate L-F) **state of creating dissension or discord**

divisive

"If you create these profit centers, and it creates **divisiveness** and the profit of one is a result of a loss of another, you don't benefit the corporation."
> — Willard C. Butcher, Chairman and CEO, Chase Manhattan Bank, N.A., in *Across the Board*

By encouraging cooperation and knowledge-sharing, Jamal sought to overcome the **divisive** mood in the company.

divulge (*vulgare* to make known L) **tell, reveal, make known**

You shouldn't **divulge** this information to anyone but the company president.

Doctors and lawyers are protected by law from **divulging** confidential information about their clients.

dynamic (*dynasthai* to be able G-F) **energetic, forceful**

dynamically
dynamism

Donna, our CEO, seeks a workforce that is **dynamic** and always ready with fresh ideas.

The chairman's **dynamism** was manifested in his high energy level and creative ideas.

- QUIZ -

Match the Tier II word in the first column with its synonym in the
second column.

_____	1. disseminate	a.	belittle
_____	2. divisiveness	b.	uneven
_____	3. dissuade	c.	energetic
_____	4. dissipate	d.	discourage
_____	5. disproportionate	e.	scatter
_____	6. disparage	f.	tell
_____	7. divulge	g.	difference
_____	8. dynamic	h.	state of discord
_____	9. disparity	i.	spread widely

Answers:

1. i	4. e	6. a	8. c
2. h	5. b	7. f	9. g
3. d			

Review Letter D

Without referring to the previous chapter, identify the synonyms of the italicized words.

PART A

1. Showing much *tact*, the supervisor complimented Joe's outstanding job without making the others feel inferior. d_____

2. The accusations of impropriety ended in a *disaster* for the arms exporter. d_____

3. Lucy's cheerful *outward manner* hid the sadness she was feeling. d_____

4. The president encountered a *sharp split* between those who wanted a quick fix for the economy and those who preferred gradual growth. d_____

5. The personnel department's plan to cancel the pension plan was a *very bad* idea, and it was forced to recant. d_____

6. My advice is to make your case clearly and not to *ramble*. d_____

7. The accusations of harassment were certainly *harmful* to the candidate's campaign. d_____

8. No one could *discourage* Frank from his determination to write the Great American Novel. d_____

9. We were delighted to find no *difference* between our actual and budgeted expenses. d_____

10. I did not *detect* any imperfections in the textile samples. d_____

11. The color key is intended to help you *contrast* the similar shades of blue. d_____

PART B

1. In a job interview, it's important to show that you are *energetic* and hardworking. d_____

2. The jury hopes to make a *conclusive* decision by the end of the day. d_____

3. A recession is likely to *weaken* the recreation industries, such as travel and sporting goods. d_____

4. Faced with the *difficult choice* of dieting versus exercise, Ted opted for a combination. d_____

5. The picnic was resumed when the clouds began to *scatter*. d_____

6. The department endured a period of *disorder* after the staff reorganization. d_____

7. Harry thought the best way to get the contract was to *put down* his competitor's track record. d_____

8. My respect for Arlene's artistic talent will never *lessen*. d_____

9. Public trust of government has continued to *worsen* over the past few decades. d_____

10. The onset of the computer age hastened the *death* of the typewriter company. d_____

PART C

1. We had a provocative *discussion*. d_____

2. Don't *reveal* any information that could jeopardize this sensitive mission. d_____

3. Before we begin, we must *define* the project's components. d_____

4. The CEO did not *pick* a successor before his retirement. d_____

5. I was embarrassed to learn that Vincent had *badmouthed* my work in front of the boss. d_____

6. After two months of graduate school, I found myself *unhappy* with the program. d_____

7. Smoking has been proven to be *harmful* to your health. d_____

8. Auto pollution is just one *aspect* of a complex environmental problem. d_____

9. The vast rewards of this job are *unequal* to the minimal amount of effort it requires. d_____

10. Mrs. McFee has asked me to *spread* the information about our building's fire safety procedures. d_____

11. The sales incentive plan caused *discord* in the retail department. d_____

Answers

A.
1. discretion
2. debacle
3. demeanor
4. dichotomy
5. deplorable
6. digress
7. deleterious/ detrimental
8. dissuade
9. disparity
10. discern
11. differentiate

B.
1. dynamic
2. definitive
3. debilitate
4. dilemma
5. dissipate
6. disarray
7. denigrate/ disparage
8. diminish
9. deteriorate
10. demise

C.
1. dialogue
2. divulge
3. delineate
4. designate
5. denigrated/ disparaged
6. disenchanted
7. detrimental/ deleterious
8. dimension
9. disproportionate
10. disseminate
11. divisiveness

- E -

elect (*legere* to choose L) **choose, decide**
election
elective

> The company has **elected** to enter the biotechnology market with an acquisition rather than from start-up.

> Eric **elected** to move with the company in its relocation rather than look for a new job in this uncertain job market.

elicit (*elicere* to elicit L) **draw out, bring to light; evoke**

> By flattering him, Marcia was able to **elicit** the answers to her questions from the reluctant witness.

> Without providing too much information, the trainer tried to **elicit** the correct responses to her questions.

elusive (*ludere* to play L) **hard-to-get, slippery; shifty, hard to pin down**
elude

> Despite our efforts, achieving a high level of profits has been a very **elusive** goal.

> By concentrating their promotion campaign on retirees, the audiocassette makers finally achieved the profits that had been **eluding** them.

embryonic (*bryein* to swell G) **beginning, undeveloped, developing**

> "Control Data invests in Business and Technology Centers, which provide **embryonic** businesses with facilities and services for much less than they'd pay elsewhere."
> — William C. Norris, Chairman, Control Data Corp., in *Across the Board*

> **Embryonic** companies are faced with different kinds of challenges than older companies.

empathy (*pathos* suffering, passion G) **sympathetic understanding**
empathic
empathically

> The best supervisors are able to show **empathy** for those under them without becoming too involved in employees' personal problems.

> As a former salesperson, Jake was very **empathic** toward the new recruits as they began their first day in the field.

emphatic (*phanein* to show G) **forceful, insistent**
emphatically

> Horatio was **emphatic** in warning us against risking too much money on the new venture.

> Although George **emphatically** stated that the business deal in Iran would be a mistake, he received no support from the marketing staff.

emulate (*aemulari* to emulate L) **strive to equal; imitate with a view to outdo**
emulation
emulative

> Because she admired and wanted to become more like Enid, Rachel **emulated** her down to the last detail.

> Joe's **emulation** of Jeff was so great that he strove to fill his shoes after Jeff left the company.

enamored (of/with) (*amour* love OF) **in love with, crazy about (colloq.)**

> "Frankly, the two founders are not very **enamored** with the past."
> > — John A. Young, President and CEO, Hewlett-Packard Co., in *Across the Board*

> Although employees like the idea, management is not usually **enamored** with giving health benefits to part-time workers.

endorse (*dorsum* back L-F) **approve, support, OK**
endorsement

"I think it's amusing that the administration first warmly
endorses the Rostenkowski proposal and then proceeds to
reject every specific one of his proposals."
> — Sen. James Sasser (D–TN), on CBS News' *Face The
> Nation*

To win an election, politicians often seek the **endorsement** of
newspapers and other elected officials.

enhance (*altus* high L) **increase, improve, heighten**
enhancement

"It's been a deliberate program to **enhance** the value of our
shares for stockholders."
> — Clifton C. Garvin, Jr., Chairman, Exxon Corp. in *Fortune*

The **enhancement** of the company's image was achieved
through good public relations coupled with an actual
improvement in the quality of their products.

enumerate (*numerare* to count L) **list, specify, detail**
enumeration

Only a fraction of a man's virtues should be **enumerated** in
his presence.
> — The Talmud

Before a space shuttle flight, an **enumeration** is made of all
items to be taken on board so that nothing is left behind.

envision (*videre* to see L-F) **see, imagine, picture**

"What do we really **envision** in Eastern Europe?"
> — Sam Nunn (D–GA), on NBC News' *Meet the Press*

When the architect looked at the unsightly railroad tracks
next to the river, he **envisioned** a park to cover them up.

ephemeral (*eip* over + *hemera* a day G) **short-lived, transient**

Spring is the most **ephemeral** season in New York; no sooner
has it arrived than summer takes over.

Todd and his family relocated so many times that, at best,
they could only develop **ephemeral** relationships with
neighbors.

- QUIZ -

Match the Tier II word in the first column with its synonym in the second column.

_____	1. enamored (with)	a. decide
_____	2. elect	b. hard to get
_____	3. empathy	c. imitate
_____	4. elusive	d. forceful
_____	5. endorse	e. understanding
_____	6. enumerate	f. short-lived
_____	7. embryonic	g. draw out
_____	8. emulate	h. in love (with)
_____	9. ephemeral	i. imagine
_____	10. emphatic	j. developing
_____	11. envision	k. improve
_____	12. elicit	l. support
_____	13. enhance	m. list

Answers:

1. h	5. l	8. c	11. i
2. a	6. m	9. f	12. g
3. e	7. j	10. d	13. k
4. b			

equilibrium (*aequi* equal + *libra* weight L) **balance**
equilibrate

> Prices seem to have stabilized, reflecting an **equilibrium** in the marketplace.

> In controlling interest rates, the Federal Reserve bank tries to **equilibrate** the need for economic growth with the desire to keep inflation down.

equivocate (*aequi* + *vox* voice L) **evade, waffle**
equivocal
equivocation

Henry **equivocated** when asked why he wanted a transfer out of the company headquarters; clearly he didn't want to burn any bridges.

When asked which candidate she liked better, Gail was **equivocal,** because she couldn't really decide between them.

erode (*rodere* to gnaw L) **wear away or be worn away, chew away; destroy or be destroyed**
erosion

Our competition's market position has been **eroded** because of our superior technology and lower costs.

We didn't realize that the **erosion** of the dollar's value would cause such a large decline in overseas travel.

erroneous (*erro* wanderer L) **wrong, mistaken, incorrect**
The "experts" were **erroneous** in thinking we could not solve our company's problems.

Ms. Clarke's statistics were **erroneous**; when we repeated her study, we developed different results.

euphemism (*eu* good + *pheme* speech G) **substitution of an inoffensive word for a more unpleasant one**
euphemistic

The executive's statement to the press was filled with **euphemisms**, but most analysts realized the company was in trouble financially.

Al, our company economist, was being **euphemistic** when he said the economy had some softness; he really meant that we are entering a depression.

euphoria (*eu* good + *pherein* to bear G) **elation, joy, bliss**
euphoric

"We all got caught up in the **euphoria** of Wall Street, buyouts and conspicuous consumption."
— Lee Iacocca, Chairman and CEO, Chrysler Corp., on CBS News' *Face the Nation*

At the first sign of an economic upturn, a wave of **euphoria** swept the country.

evolve (*volvere* to roll L) **develop, grow**
evolution

> "Our competitive environment has **evolved** into one of
> worldwide scope, where companies with hardworking and
> talented people are vying for a share of the market."
> — Dr. Ronald H. Yocum, President, USI Division,
>   Quantum Chemical Corp., in *CPI Purchasing*

Alice noted that the **evolution** of our marketing strategy had
come about through trial and error.

exacerbate (*acer* sharp L) **worsen**
exacerbation

> The oil shortage **exacerbated** an already weak economy and
> caused a recession.

> The government's decision to send in the troops caused an
> **exacerbation** of the tensions, and fighting soon began.

execute (*sequi* to follow L-F) **do, carry out, perform**
execution

> Wisdom is knowing what to do next; virtue is **executing** it.
> — Anonymous

> Jane's marketing strategy was good, but her **execution** of the
> advertising campaign was outstanding.

expire (*spirare* to breathe L-F) **end, cease, run out (colloq.)**
expiration

> "I'm hoping that we can close some loopholes and extend
> some taxes that would be **expiring**."
> — Rep. Dan Rostenkowski (D–IL), on ABC News' *This
>   Week with David Brinkley*

> We must remember to renew our operating license before its
> **expiration**.

explicit (*plicare* to fold L-F) **clear, definite, specific**
explicitly

"You can honor the principle of need [for Social Security] without putting on an **explicit** needs test."
>   — Peter Peterson, Chairman, The Blackstone Group and former Secretary of Commerce, on ABC News' *This Week with David Brinkley*

The director stated **explicitly** that all staff members would receive cost-of-living raises in the spring.

external (*exterus* being on the outside L) **outer, outside, outward**
externalization
externally

Please concern yourself only with the future of your own department, and leave it to the division vice president to consider **external** issues.

Let's proofread the new brochure inside the company but have it printed **externally**.

extricate (*tricae* trifles, perplexities L) **release, disengage, get out of**
inextricable (ant.)

A touch of folly is needed, if we are to **extricate** ourselves successfully from the hazards of life.
>   — La Rochefoucauld, French writer, 1613–1680

The issue of profit improvement is **inextricably** tied to raising prices, lowering costs or both.

- QUIZ -

Match the Tier II word in the first column with its synonym in the second column.

_____	1. euphoria	a.	carry out
_____	2. equivocate	b.	run out
_____	3. extricate	c	joy
_____	4. exacerbate	d.	waffle
_____	5. expire	e.	clear
_____	6. erode	f.	worsen
_____	7. external	g.	get out of
_____	8. evolve	h.	balance
_____	9. explicit	i.	wear away
_____	10. equilibrium	j.	outside
_____	11. execute	k.	develop
_____	12. euphemism	l.	incorrect
_____	13. erroneous	m.	substituting a mild expression for a harsh one

Answers:

1. c	5. b	8. k	11. a
2. d	6. i	9. e	12. m
3. g	7. j	10. h	13. l
4. f			

- F -

facilitate (*facere* to do L-F) **make easier, simplify**

facilitator
facility

The new database **facilitates** identifying new acquisition candidates.

Ellen is elected **facilitator** at each staff meeting, because she knows Roberts Rules of Order by heart.

fictitious (*fingere* to shape L) **made up, imaginary, false**
fiction
fictitiously

> By creating **fictitious** companies and characters, the participants in the role-playing session were better able to confront their real organizational problems.

> Certain newspapers thrive on publishing stories which are not only **fictitious** but highly improbable.

flagrant (*flagrare* to burn L) **obviously bad, outrageous, glaring**
flagrantly

> The securities violations were so **flagrant** that Congress felt obligated to enact stiffer penalties for future crimes.

> Liz **flagrantly** ignored the no-smoking signs, and soon an angry crowd had assembled outside her office to scold her.

flourish (*flos* flower L-F) **thrive, succeed, do well**

> If our democracy is to **flourish**, it must have criticism; if our government is to function, it must have dissent.
> — Henry Steele Commager, American educator, 1902–1984

> Jerry was a failure as a salesperson, but he **flourished** as a financial manager.

fluctuate (*fluctus* flow, wave L) **vary, change**
fluctuation

> Program trading causes stock market prices to **fluctuate** widely.

> Temporary employment agencies thrive on the **fluctuation** of work in many offices.

formidable (*formido* fear L) **tough, powerful, difficult**
formidably

> "Do we try to help the Russians avoid collapse, in which event they turn out to be a more **formidable** antagonist, or do we let them collapse?"
> — Sen. Daniel P. Moynihan (D–NY), on ABC News' *This Week with David Brinkley*

The Democratic candidate argued her position **formidably**, and in the end she was the victor.

formulate   (*forma* form L)   **put together, plan, devise**
formula
formulation

Ann, have you **formulated** an advertising budget?

I fear that we're beginning this project without having clearly **formulated** our purpose and methodology.

fundamental   (*fundare* to found L)   **basic, underlying**
fundamentally

> "It's a **fundamental** moral test for society—whether it is willing to invest some of its own resources now for the benefit of those yet to come."
>> — Richard G. Darman, Director, Office of Management and Budget, on CBS News' *Face the Nation*

One of the **fundamental** reasons for our success as a company has been our integrity.

- G -

galvanize   (*fr. Luigi Galvani* I)   **stimulate, excite, arouse**

The increase in market share was **galvanized** by Murray's innovative sales and advertising program.

It shouldn't be difficult to **galvanize** the staff in support of the walk-a-thon.

generic   (*genus* birth, class L-F)   **common, general**
generically

> "The CEC [Corporate Executive Council] also deals with **generic** issues that cut across all sectors."
>> — Michael Carpenter, CEO, Kidder, Peabody & Co., Inc., in *Planning Review*

Although the advertising strategy was originally planned **generically**, we later tailored it to the specific requirements of an engineering firm.

- H -

harbinger (*herberge* hostlery, innkeeping Gmc-F) **sign, omen, forerunner**

> A rising or falling stock market is usually a **harbinger** of a growing or faltering economy.

> The congressman argued that an arms buildup could only be a **harbinger** of war.

humiliation (*humilis* low L) **embarrassment, shame, disgrace**
humiliate

> It has always been a mystery to me how men can feel themselves honored by the **humiliation** of their fellow beings.
> — Mohandas K. Gandhi

> I know you were embarrassed when Kate criticized your logo design, but I'm sure she never intended to **humiliate** you.

hypothetical (*hypo* under + *tithenai* to put G) **supposed; assumed**
hypothesis

> We could **hypothetically** double our market share in three years if we spent enough money for new equipment and more salesmen.

> Larry tested his **hypothesis** that the recession was over by interviewing CEOs about their recent sales and hiring trends.

- QUIZ -

Match the Tier II word in the first column with its synonym in the second column.

_____	1. flagrant	a.	tough
_____	2. fundamental	b.	change
_____	3. formidable	c.	arouse
_____	4. generic	d.	outrageous
_____	5. fictitious	e.	basic
_____	6. galvanize	f.	omen
_____	7. flourish	g.	make easier
_____	8. harbinger	h.	common
_____	9. formulate	i.	shame
_____	10. facilitate	j.	do well
_____	11. humiliation	k.	plan
_____	12. fluctuate	l.	supposed
_____	13. hypothetical	m.	false

Answers:

1. d	5. m	8. f	11. i
2. e	6. c	9. k	12. b
3. a	7. j	10. g	13. l
4. h			

Review Letters E-F-G-H

Choose the word in this chapter that most closely approximates the following italicized Tier I word.

PART A

1. Losing your temper will just *worsen* the problem. e_____

2. Many people find their weight tends to *vary* with the seasons. f_____

3. No one would have predicted that Mary would *decide* to study biology in college. e_____

4. The chairman of the board is trying to *stimulate* enthusiasm for the relocation to the sunbelt. g_____

5. The blooming crocus is thought to be a *sign* that spring is soon to come. h_____

6. Because she could *imagine* a career as a graphic designer, Carmen was very successful in art school. e_____

7. Her co-workers thought that Lois's vacation adventure story was *made up* until they saw the photographs. f_____

8. Raoul's interest in skateboarding was *transient*; within a week he had discovered skydiving. e_____

9. Bill had to *disengage* the telephone wires from the knot of computer cords to find out whether the printer had come unplugged. e_____

10. Carl watched his employer *develop* from a "mom and pop" store into a Fortune 500 company. e_____

11. It shouldn't be very hard to replace this *common* bolt. g_____

12. It was difficult to *draw out* any information from the lost child. e_____

13. We can *improve* the quality of this product without having to raise the price. e_____

14. Anthony's *joy* was apparent from the huge grin on his face.
     e_____

PART B

1. I received *clear* instructions to wait for Mike at the garage.
    e_____

2. Adding a children's book division helped the publishing
    house achieve a sense of *balance.* e_____

3. My faced turned red from the *shame* I felt. h_____

4. In changing jobs, I sought a challenge and ignored what I
    considered *outside* issues, such as salary. e_____

5. Vera had all the spunk she needed to *thrive* as an attorney.
    f_____

6. Mr. Lewis overcame *difficult* obstacles to come to this
    country. f_____

7. The newlyweds are *crazy about* each other. e_____ (with)

8. Have you chosen a candidate to *support* in the next mayoral
    race? e_____

9. My figures were *wrong*, so my calculator must have been
    broken. e_____

10. The *glaring* grammatical error in the brochure was
    embarrassing. f_____

11. Larry used a *supposed* example to illustrate his point.
    h_____

12. My disorientation at my new job was *short-lived*; within
    weeks I had gotten used to the daily routine.
    e_____

13. An understanding of geometry is *basic* to an architect.
    f_____

14. Sylvia tries to *imitate* her boss with an eye to impressing her.
    e_____

PART C

1. Peg thought she would avoid insulting me by using *inoffensive
    words in place of harsh ones.* e_____

2. The travel agency staff had to *list* the reasons to visit
    Scandinavia. e_____

3. Gregory was *forceful* in his endorsement of John for mayor.
    e_____

4. Your skills in chess will certainly *change* over time.
    e_____

5. Having once taken a strong stand on the issue of trade barriers, John is now *evasive* about his opinion. e_____

6. The opportunity to purchase inexpensive airplane tickets will soon *run out.* e_____

7. Tony learned of the toxic spill just before the meeting; he only had minutes to *put together* an explanation. f_____

8. The competition is *wearing away* our position. e_____

9. With the help of volunteers, the archaeologists were able to *carry out* the excavation in a short time. e_____

10. The health-care plan was in an *early* stage. e_____

11. Barbara found that, with the new on-line help function, even complex tasks were *made easier.* f_____

12. Success can be very *hard to get.* e_____

13. Michael seemed to treat his partner's problem with *sympathetic understanding.* e_____

Answers

A.
1. exacerbate
2. fluctuate
3. elect
4. galvanize
5. harbinger
6. envision
7. fictitious
8. ephemeral
9. extricate
10. evolve
11. generic
12. elicit
13. enhance
14. euphoria

B.
1. explicit
2. equilibrium
3. humiliation
4. external
5. flourish
6. formidable
7. enamored
8. endorse
9. erroneous
10. flagrant
11. hypothetical
12. ephemeral
13. fundamental
14. emulate

C.
1. euphemisms
2. enumerate
3. emphatic
4. evolve
5. equivocal
6. expire
7. formulate
8. eroding
9. execute
10. embryonic
11. facilitated
12. elusive
13. empathy

- I -

illusion (*ludere* to mock L-F) **false belief, fantasy, "pipe dream"**
disillusion
illusory

> One day all will be well, that is our hope; all's well today, that
> is our **illusion**.
> — Voltaire

> After dreaming of quick profits, Irene was **disillusioned** when
> she saw the stock price go down sharply.

illustrate (*lustrare* to make bright L) **show, demonstrate**
illustration
illustrative

> "I think it's probably not correct to say that Iran controls the
> hostage holders; they certainly have very strong influence on
> them, as the French hostage release **illustrates** this past week."
> — Rep. Lee Hamilton (D–IN), on CBS News' *Face The
> Nation*

> The corporation's decision to move to the sunbelt is
> **illustrative** of a national trend.

imminent (*imminere* to threaten L) **about to occur, near, close at
hand**
imminence
imminently

> A final decision about whether or not we close the
> manufacturing site is **imminent**.

> The **imminence** of the snow storm caused the stock market to
> be closed several hours early.

impair (*pejorare* to make worse L-F) **hurt, harm, weaken**
impairment

Undoubtedly the new regulations will **impair** our competition's ability to compete because they have not prepared for the changes as we have.

Although the retail clothing industry has been showing signs of **impairment** for some time, a large women's store just opened a branch in our neighborhood.

impediment (*ped* foot L) **barrier, obstacle, stumbling block**
impede

Language differences create an **impediment** for Americans doing business in China.

Despite the council member's being found innocent on a bribery charge, the public's lingering distrust of him will be an **impediment** to his reelection.

imperative (*imperare* to command L) **necessity, requirement; necessary**

"Quality performance is an economic **imperative**."
— Dr. Ronald H. Yocum, President, USI Division, Quantum Chemical Corp., in *CPI Purchasing*

Even though the director knows you were sick on Tuesday, it is **imperative** that you make note of your absence on your time sheet.

imperil (*peira* trial, experiment G) **endanger, risk**

Introducing a new drug without testing it would **imperil** the safety of all consumers.

The company's future was **imperiled** by the rapid growth of its competitor.

impetus (*petere* to go to L) **motivation, stimulus**

"I think there is a much greater **impetus** to the economy by savings and getting the interest rates down [than by cutting capital gains taxes]."
— Sen. Lloyd Bentsen (D–TX), on CBS News' *Face The Nation*

What was Carla's **impetus** for changing her vote at the last minute?

implausible (*plaudere* to applaud L) **unlikely, dubious, doubtful, hard to believe**

implausibility

> The more **implausible** a slander is, the better fools remember it.
> — Casimir Delavigne, French poet, 1793–1843

Her supervisor was put off by the **implausibility** of Sally's explanation for her lateness.

implement (*plere* to fill L) **carry out, fulfill, execute**

implementation

> "Tenacity is as important as your strategy because when you **implement** a radical plan, I guarantee you, everything bad that can happen will happen."
> — Charles S. Sanford, Jr., President, Bankers Trust Co., in *Planning Review*

This marketing strategy looks good on paper, but we won't know if it's good until its **implementation**.

implicit (*plicare* to fold L) **understood, unspoken**

implicitly
implication

> "Like many other large companies in the United States, Europe and Japan, GE has had an **implicit** psychological contract based on perceived lifetime employment."
> — John F. Welch, Jr., Chairman and CEO, General Electric Corp., in *Harvard Business Review*

Although the President would not admit planning a tax hike, we knew **implicitly** that taxes would have to rise to carry out his program.

implore (*plorare* to wail L-F) **beg, plead with, appeal to**

I **implored** our company president to reconsider our proposal for a new advertising program; when he reconsidered, he approved the program.

When the volume of George's radio began to distract me from my work, I **implored** him to purchase earphones.

- QUIZ -

Match the Tier II word in the first column with its synonym in the second column.

_____ 1. illustrate	a. near
_____ 2. imperative	b. understood
_____ 3. implicit	c. show
_____ 4. imperil	d. beg
_____ 5. implausible	e. necessity
_____ 6. imminent	f. risk
_____ 7. implement	g. obstacle
_____ 8. impair	h. doubtful
_____ 9. implore	i. fantasy
_____ 10. impediment	j. weaken
_____ 11. impetus	k. fulfill
_____ 12. illusion	l. motivation

Answers:

1. c	4. f	7. k	10. g
2. e	5. h	8. j	11. l
3. b	6. a	9. d	12. i

---

impoverish (*pauper* poor L-F) **to make poor, reduce to poverty**
impoverishment

> Having come from an **impoverished** home, Janet was determined to be a success.

> The corporation decided not to close the plant, because such a move would **impoverish** much of the small company town.

inadvertent (*advertere* to turn [the mind] to L) **accidental, negligent, inattentive**
inadvertently
inadvertence

> Fatigue from lack of sleep was a factor in Jeff's **inadvertent** pushing of the fire alarm button.

Not paying attention to the stop sign, Sheila **inadvertently** bumped into the car in front of her.

inception *(capere to take L)* beginning, start, onset

"A business team was formed at the **inception** of the project."
— John G. Smale, Chairman and CEO, Procter & Gamble Co., in *Across the Board*

Mechanisms for quality control should be considered at the **inception** of the project—before it's too late.

inconceivable *(concipere to conceive L)* unbelievable, incredible

conceivable (ant.)
conceivably (ant.)
inconceivability
inconceivably

Because he didn't believe in luck, it was **inconceivable** to Rob that he would ever win the lottery.

While a wristwatch computer was technically **conceivable**, from a marketing perspective, the idea did not hold much promise.

incongruity *(congruere to come together L)* inconsistency, discrepancy; unsuitability, inappropriateness

incongruous

There is an **incongruity** that we need to understand: our division's sales increased dramatically while the economy slowed.

Joyce's actions are **incongruous** with her instructions to others; she doesn't practice what she preaches.

inconsequential *(consequi to follow along L)* petty, small, unimportant, insignificant

Our analysis of the project proves that the risks are **inconsequential**.

Although the tiny decimal point appears **inconsequential**, its placement is tremendously important in mathematics.

incredulous (*credere* to believe L) **unbelieving, disbelieving, doubting, skeptical**
incredulity
incredulously

> The plant engineer was simply **incredulous** when he was informed that impurities had found their way into the products at this facility.

> When the jury found her assailant not guilty, Dolores couldn't hide her **incredulity**.

incumbent (on or upon) (*cumbere* to lie down on L) **obligatory for, required of; a person who holds an office**

> It is **incumbent** upon those in the chemical industry to take the lead in developing novel ways of handling the pollution problem.

> The **incumbent** senator hoped to keep his seat in Congress for six more years.

indigenous (*gignere* to beget L) **native, natural**

> Oil is **indigenous** to Texas.

> When the company announced plans to build a plant in a less industrialized country, it announced that not only the labor force but also upper management would be drawn from the **indigenous** population.

indispensable (*dispendere* to weigh out L) **necessary, essential, vital**
dispensable (ant.)

> It seems that having a computer is as **indispensable** for an engineer today as a calculator was ten years ago.

> As the newest and least experienced member of the team, he is the most **dispensable** if layoffs are necessary.

indoctrinate (*docere* to teach L-F) **instruct; brainwash, teach uncritically**
indoctrination

> When Art joined the company, he was immediately **indoctrinated** with the company's basic philosophy and rules.

Checks and balances are an **inherent** part of our system of government.

inimical   (*inimicus* enemy L)   **harmful, unfavorable; hostile**

The president feels that a friendly takeover would not be **inimical** to the company's future success.

Being so dependent on one large customer could be **inimical** to the long term health of our company.

initiate   (*ire* to go L)   **begin, start**

initiation
initiative
initiator

Ruth has **initiated** the most detailed study of our transportation costs that we have ever undertaken.

The paper flow proceeded much faster after the **initiation** of new procedures for approval of projects.

innocuous   (*nocere* to harm L)   **harmless**

It seemed like an **innocuous** joke to us, but Jack was very much offended by it.

The salesperson said that a slight rise in the cost of steel will have an **innocuous** effect; we don't expect our customers to cancel their orders because of it.

innuendo   (*nuere* to nod L)   **derogatory reference, suggestion, hint**

"I'm saying that you should establish criminal intent, and it shouldn't just be [based on] **innuendos** and half-truths."
—   Sen. Orrin Hatch (R–UT), on ABC News' *This Week with David Brinkley*

Since Gary is usually very upbeat and forthright, I was very surprised to hear his sarcastic comments and **innuendos**.

inordinate   (*ordinare* to arrange L)   **excessive, unreasonable, unwarranted**

inordinately

Albert seemed to spend an **inordinate** amount of time on that portion of the analysis, but the results were brilliant.

The boss prepared me for a tough assignment, but it wasn't **inordinately** difficult.

inscrutable (*scrutari* to search L) **mysterious, unknowable**

Our manager's strategy for gaining market share by developing specialty markets is highly profitable yet **inscrutable** to the competition.

The chairman guarded his private life so completely that it was basically **inscrutable**.

instigate (*stigare* to urge on L) **trigger, start; provoke, arouse**
instigation
instigator

The president's decision to begin widescale layoffs **instigated** an immediate protest by employees whose jobs were at stake.

Gretchen was concerned that a similar product had already been developed, so at her **instigation** the company launched a patent search.

intangible (*tangere* to touch L-F) **vague, indefinable; subtle; abstract**
intangibly
intangibility
tangible (ant.)

"The third level of extrapolation is what I think you are talking about—concepts of grandeur and greatness, and the more **intangible** qualities of life."
— Willard C. Butcher, Chairman and CEO, The Chase Manhattan Bank, N.A., in *Across the Board*

He set more store in **intangible** virtue than in hard cash.

integrate (*tangere* to touch L) **combine, blend, unite, put together**
integration
disintegrate (ant.)
disintegration

"The risk was in managing the software, in **integrating** our information system with our control system."
— J. Tracy O'Rourke, President and CEO, Allen-Bradley Co., in *Harvard Business Review*

Our public relations department has benefitted greatly from its **integration** with the marketing staff.

- QUIZ -

Match the Tier II word in the first column with its synonym in the second column.

_____	1. infuriated	a. naturally
_____	2. inherently	b. combine
_____	3. inimical	c. provoke
_____	4. initiate	d. angered
_____	5. innocuous	e. mysterious
_____	6. innuendo	f. begin
_____	7. inordinate	g. vague
_____	8. inscrutable	h. unfavorable
_____	9. instigate	i. excessive
_____	10. intangible	j. hint
_____	11. integrate	k. harmless

Answers:

1. d	4. f	7. i	10. g
2. a	5. k	8. e	11. b
3. h	6. j	9. c	

---

intensify (*intendere* to stretch out L-F) **increase, strengthen, heighten, sharpen**

intense
intensity
intensive

> "The diversion of funds to the Contras **intensified** as time went on, but it was there from the outset."
> — Sen. Daniel P. Moynihan (D–NY), in *The New York Times*

The competition among electronics dealers is **intense**, which leads to frequent price cuts in the industry.

interim (*inter* between L) **interval, meantime**

> "In the **interim**, some real estate values will begin to suffer, and perhaps be bailed out by a more inflationary push next year."
>> — Henry Kaufman, Partner and Chief Economist, Salomon Brothers Inc., in *Across the Board*

> Soon we will hire a full-time secretary; in the **interim** salespersons will have to type their own correspondence.

intermittent (*mittere* to send L) **periodic, irregular, off-and-on**

intermittently

> We have experienced long but **intermittent** periods of growth in sales, the cause of which we need to understand.

> Our store sells a steady 1,000 watches per month, but sales of umbrellas rise **intermittently**, depending on the weather.

intervene (*venire* to come L) **step in, get involved; mediate; come between, interfere**

intervention

> "It was also a responsibility for us to have forces deployed [so that], if a decision were made to **intervene** militarily, we could do so."
>> — Richard Cheney, Secretary of Defense, on CBS News' *Face the Nation*

> Do you think that the government should take a back-seat role in environmental regulation, or do you believe in greater **intervention**?

intimidate (*timere* to fear L) **frighten, bully, scare**

intimidation

> [Atomic energy] may **intimidate** the human race into bringing order into its international affairs.
>> — Albert Einstein

> Most managers, in dealing with their employees, try to create a climate of trust and mutual respect instead of an atmosphere of **intimidation**.

intolerable (*tolerare* to put up with L) **unbearable, excessive**

intolerance
intolerant
tolerable (ant.)
tolerant (ant.)

> "Reforming COLAs [Cost of Living Adjustments] would impose an **intolerable** burden on the people."
> — Peter Peterson, Chairman, The Blackstone Group and former Secretary of Commerce, on ABC News' *This Week with David Brinkley*

Mr. Lawrence hired an inspector because of his **intolerance** for defective products.

intractable (*tractare* to draw violently, handle, treat L) **not easily led, uncontrollable, unmanageable, stubborn**

intractability
intractably

> Low employee morale and inefficient bureaucracy were two **intractable** problems that had long plagued the company.

> Increasing the cash flow will not come easily or quickly because of the **intractability** of the basic debt problem.

intransigent (*trans* across + *agere* to drive L) **stubborn, inflexible, unyielding, unbending**

intransigence
intransigently

> They were surprisingly **intransigent** about the contract's starting date, although they had been quite reasonable about the provisions.

> By refusing to hear last-minute testimony from the prosecution, the judge showed great **intransigence**.

intrinsic (*intrinsecus* inward, on the inside L) **native, natural, real**

intrinsically

> Elizabeth was an **intrinsic** part of the company's team, and when she left the company, the loss was deeply felt.

The **intrinsic** value of the company, based on its vast real estate holdings, was much greater than most investors realized.

intuition (*tueri* to look at L) **sense, feeling, natural instinct; hunch (informal)**

intuitive

"The results of this (planning) analysis were very clear and matched our own **intuition**."
> — Paul E. Lego, President and COO, Westinghouse Electric Corp., in *Planning Review*

The clients said that Martha was remarkably **intuitive**; when she unveiled the advertising campaign, they thought she had read their minds.

invalidate (*valere* to be strong L) **disprove, negate, nullify, destroy, ruin (colloq.)**

invalid
valid (ant.)
validate (ant.)

Because of mistakes in the voting procedure, the National Labor Relations Board **invalidated** the results of the union election.

When the state outlawed smoking in public buildings, our own office policy became **invalid**.

invincible (*vincere* to conquer L-F) **unconquerable; powerful, very secure**

invincibility

His financial success made him feel **invincible**.

Deborah's sense of **invincibility** led her to leverage the company's assets on the stock market.

irony (*eiron* dissembler G) **events that are the opposite of what is expected; ridicule, light sarcasm**

ironic
ironical

"I think you have the supreme **irony** . . . [CIA Director William] Casey once suggested to him that [Colonel Oliver] North might be too junior to be the fall guy."
> — Sen. George J. Mitchell (D–ME), on ABC News' *This Week with David Brinkley*

It's **ironic** that the business division that was the weakest three years ago is now the strongest, whereas the division, which was by far the strongest, is now the weakest.

irrevocable (*re* back, again + *vocare* to call L) **incapable of being changed or undone, unchangeable, final**
  irrevocably

The XYZ Company's decision to relocate is **irrevocable** despite the complaints of many employees.

My reputation as a top accountant was **irrevocably** damaged when I made an error in the annual report.

issue (*ire* to go L-F) **question, topic, subject**
  "The leadership has not been there on this **issue** [deficit reduction], either from the President or the Congress."
> — Rep. Leon Panetta (D–CA), on NBC News' *Meet The Press*

How to assure both a solid job base and a sound environment are two **issues** on the agenda of many companies today.

- QUIZ -

Match the Tier II word in the first column with its synonym(s) in the second column.

_____ 1. intermittent	a. not easily led
_____ 2. intimidate	b. get involved
_____ 3. irrevocable	c. sense
_____ 4. intensify	d. stubborn
_____ 5. invalidate	e. meantime
_____ 6. intervene	f. topic
_____ 7. intransigent	g. irregular
_____ 8. intuition	h. negate
_____ 9. intractable	i. unbearable
_____ 10. intrinsic	j. heighten
_____ 11. intolerable	k. powerful
_____ 12. interim	l. opposite of what is expected
_____ 13. issue	m. unchangeable
_____ 14. invincible	n. natural
_____ 15. irony	o. frighten

Answers:

1. g	5. h	9. a, d	13. f
2. o	6. b	10. n	14. k
3. m	7. d, a	11. i	15. l
4. j	8. c	12. e	

Review Letter I

Write the appropriate higher-level word that is synonymous with the italicized words below.

PART A

1. A parking ticket is a minor *violation* of the law. i_____

2. "Women in Business" was the *topic* discussed at the roundtable. i_____

3. If you *start* a discussion of students' rights at the board meeting, the others will join in. i_____

4. Len's participation on the committee is *irregular*. i_____

5. The search for a new kind of seat belt was *provoked* by the CEO after his car accident. i_____

6. Eliza's motives for leaving town were *mysterious*, and everyone was baffled. i_____

7. It took an hour for the rain to slow, but in the *meantime*, we played cards. i_____

8. Jill is so *stubborn*, she refuses to follow directions. i_____

9. The World Series was *unimportant* to Graham, who is not a baseball fan. i_____

10. A sense of direction is an *innate* gift. i_____

11. The snake bite turned out to be *harmless*. i_____

12. I do not drink and drive because I do not want to *endanger* myself or anyone else. i_____

13. Don't let the chairman *frighten* you; he's really a gentleman. i_____

14. Please *put together* the different parts of this report so that they read smoothly. i_____

15. Who will *carry out* the budget cuts after the president is gone? i_____

16. Liz said her toothache was *unbearable*. i_____
17. Ted was *angered* when a drunken driver smashed into his new car. i_____

PART B

1. The farmer said a drought would leave him *reduced to poverty*. i_____

2. It is *required of* us to practice what we preach. i_____ (on)

3. The jury found the witness's explanations *unlikely*. i_____

4. A dictionary is *essential* to an editor. i_____

5. Joe's bad attitude was *harmful* to our team spirit. i_____

6. The automobile emissions test is not always *foolproof*. i_____

7. Bev likes to be doted on because her parents paid an *excessive* amount of attention to her. i_____

8. Our market position is *very secure*. i_____

9. Election redistricting may *weaken* our voting strength. i_____

10. Heavy winds indicated that a storm was *about to occur*. i_____

11. Terry had to *beg* her mother for another loan. i_____

12. We were startled by the *inconsistency* in Mr. Tracey's earlier and later comments. i_____

13. The rewards of my job are *indefinable* and cannot be measured in dollars and cents. i_____

14. Lois took her complaint of *unjust* treatment to the grievance board. i_____

15. The staff was *skeptical* when they saw the sales figures for the month. i_____

16. Bob's rude comment was *accidental*. i_____

17. The economist stated that inflation was *not easily controlled*. i_____

PART C

1. Jane had no *incentive* other than kindness to do volunteer work. i_____

2. The error in this equation *nullifies* the whole theory. i_____

3. Studying grammar is a *natural* part of learning to write. (an) i_____

4. Palm trees are *native* to Florida. i_____

5. George's ego is an *obstacle* to his success. i_____

6. The staff was *instructed* in the company sales policy during the weekend retreat. i_____

7. Claire was under a *false belief* that her supervisor intended to promote her. (an) i_____

8. When we were hired, it was *understood* that we would attend the annual convention. i_____

9. Our competitor used a *derogatory reference* in speaking about our company. (an) i_____

10. The playwright frequently inserted *the opposite of what was expected*, and we were often taken off guard by the story line. i_____

11. Jane's *feeling* about the future was usually right on target. i_____

12. We had to *increase* our sales efforts at the end of the fiscal year. i_____

13. Dr. Blair used a blackboard to *show* how to organize the campaign. i_____

14. It is *necessary* to lower prices immediately or we will lose a lot of sales at Christmas time. i_____

15. Don't *get involved* in other people's problems. i_____

16. At the project's *beginning*, I was optimistic about its potential. i_____

17. The decision to close the factory was *final*. i_____

Answers

A.
1. infraction
2. issue
3. initiate
4. intermittent
5. instigate
6. inscrutable
7. interim
8. intransigent
9. inconsequential
10. inherent
11. innocuous
12. imperil
13. intimidate
14. integrate
15. implement
16. intolerable
17. infuriated

B.
1. impoverished
2. incumbent (on)
3. implausible
4. indispensable
5. inimical
6. infallible
7. inordinate
8. invincible
9. impair
10. imminent
11. implore
12. incongruity
13. intangible
14. inequitable
15. incredulous
16. inadvertent
17. intractable

C.
1. impetus
2. invalidates
3. intrinsic
4. indigenous
5. impediment
6. indoctrinated
7. illusion
8. implicit
9. innuendo
10. irony
11. intuition
12. intensify
13. illustrate
14. imperative
15. intervene
16. inception
17. irrevocable

- J -

jeopardy (*jeuparti* divided game OF) **risk, danger, endangered**
jeopardize

> "The only government that's been in **jeopardy** in the last
> seven years seems to have been our own, not the
> Nicaraguans—they're stronger today."
> > — Sen. Christopher Dodd (D–CT), on ABC News' *This
> > Week with David Brinkley*

Claudia invited the plastics salesman to the holiday party so
as not to **jeopardize** our company's relationship with him.

- L -

legacy (*legare* to send as emissary L-F) **gift, bequest, heritage**
> "The **legacy** of this administration is that it shifted us from
> being the largest creditor nation in history to being the largest
> debtor nation in history."
> > — Sen. Albert Gore, Jr. (D–TN), on ABC News' *This Week
> > with David Brinkley*

Many of the employees have worked for this company for
most of their lives, because of its **legacy** of treating employees
well.

lucrative (*lucrari* to gain L-F) **very profitable, well-paying**
After Matt signed a very **lucrative** contract, he celebrated by
purchasing a new Cadillac.

The decision to manufacture computer chips has been a very
lucrative one for a lucky few companies.

- M -

magnitude   (*magnus* great L)   **size, extent**

"I don't want to enter into another conspiracy of silence with this administration about the full **magnitude** of the deficit problem facing this country."
> — Sen. James Sasser (D–TN), on CBS News' *Face The Nation*

I never understood the **magnitude** of this project until I saw the mountain of paperwork on your desk.

malfunction   (*male* badly + *fungi* to perform L)   **work improperly, break down**

The plant equipment always seems to **malfunction** in very hot weather.

If our product is going to **malfunction** within its first year of operation, it is most likely to do so immediately after its purchase.

mandate   (*manus* hand + *dere* to put L)   **order, command; authority**

mandatory

"We had a **mandate** to use this [communications satellite] for the benefit of all the countries in the world."
> — Irving Goldstein, CEO, Comsat, in *Across the Board*

Our attendance at the awards ceremony was **mandatory**.

manifest   (*manifestus* evident L)   **show or reveal (itself), appear**

manifestation

"We identified a market for all of the **manifestations** of the technology."
> — Paul Cook, CEO, Raychem Corp., in *Harvard Business Review*

If problems arise following an acquisition, they **manifest** themselves early.

manipulate (*manus* + *plere* to fill L-F) **control, handle, influence**

manipulation
manipulative
manipulator

> Man can be scientifically **manipulated**.
> — Bertrand Russell

Working behind the scenes like a puppeteer, Nikki is an expert at the **manipulation** of people for business purposes.

meticulous (*metus* fear L) **very careful, accurate, or precise**

meticulously

> "I think the President intends to read [the Tower Commission Report on Arms for Iran] **meticulously** in order to learn what was going on."
> — Edmund Muskie, former Senator, on ABC News'
> *Nightline*

We all read the finely-printed instructions **meticulously** before operating the new photocopier.

misconstrue (*struere* to build L) **misunderstand, misinterpret, misread**

Bob **misconstrued** the president's comment and thought the company was for sale.

I hope you do not **misconstrue** my comments as criticism, because they are meant to be advice.

mitigate (*mitis* soft + *agere* to drive L) **reduce, lessen, moderate**

mitigation
unmitigated (ant.)

> "[The rapid application of oil dispersants] would have **mitigated** to some significant extent the damage that would subsequently occur [from the Valdez oil spill.]"
> — Lawrence Rawl, Chairman, Exxon Corp., on CBS News'
> *Face The Nation*

Our accountability for such poor performance in sales was **mitigated** by the fact that the economy went into a recession.

mundane (*mundus* world L-F) **down-to-earth, ordinary, routine**

Bud's not worried about the world economy; his concerns are more **mundane**, like improving his golf game.

A wide variety of tasks kept Jim's job from becoming **mundane**.

- QUIZ -

Match the Tier II word in the first column with its synonym in the second column.

_____	1. manipulate	a. profitable
_____	2. magnitude	b. ordinary
_____	3. mitigate	c. control
_____	4. manifest	d. misunderstand
_____	5. jeopardy	e. size
_____	6. legacy	f. careful
_____	7. misconstrue	g. order
_____	8. mandate	h. lessen
_____	9. malfunction	i. show
_____	10. meticulous	j. heritage
_____	11. lucrative	k. work improperly
_____	12. mundane	l. risk

Answers:

1. c	4. i	7. d	10. f
2. e	5. l	8. g	11. a
3. h	6. j	9. k	12. b

- N -

neutralize (*ne* not + *uter* which of two L) **cancel out, offset**
neutral
neutrality

The losses in the consumer division **neutralized** the profits in the chemical division.

When the chairman of the board questioned the treasurer's statistics, you were wise to remain **neutral**.

nominal (*nomen* name L) **small, slight**
nominally

Quickly returning one's business calls is a **nominal** price to pay for a reputation of reliability.

Gloria's estimate of the printing job differed only **nominally** from mine, so I didn't mind using her calculations.

- O -

obscure (*ob* over L + *scur* covered place Gmc) **unknown, unclear, confusing; not well known**
obscurity

Janice made reference in her speech to an **obscure** journal.

Frank was plucked from the **obscurity** of a secretarial job to become director of human resources.

obtain (*tenere* to hold L-F) **get, acquire**
obtainable
unobtainable (ant.)

Laura, were you able to **obtain** the information for the report?

The regulations for foam insulation are **obtainable** from the Office of Consumer and Product Safety.

ominous (*omen* omen L) **highly unfavorable, threatening, gloomy**
ominously

The economic indicators are starting to show some **ominous** trends.

Last year, the company came **ominously** close to bankruptcy, so this year its filing for Chapter 11 was no surprise.

omit (*mittere* to let go, send L) **leave out, skip**
omission

The sales manager purposely **omitted** the price from the sales contract in order to discuss it in person.

The **omission** of Bill's name from the company's softball team roster was simple to correct.

onerous (*onus* burden L-F) **difficult, burdensome, oppressive**

The workload has become so **onerous** that we will need to hire more people.

Working on the project was especially **onerous** when I had the flu, but winning the engineering account made it worthwhile.

overt (*ouvrir* to open MF) **open, obvious, public**

overtly

John could not have been more **overt** about wanting the promotion.

The commercial stated **overtly** that our client's toothpaste outshined the others.

- QUIZ -

Match the Tier II word in the first column with its synonym in the second column.

_____	1. obscure	a. leave out
_____	2. onerous	b. get
_____	3. neutralize	c. cancel out
_____	4. ominous	d. open
_____	5. overt	e. not well known
_____	6. omit	f. burdensome
_____	7. nominal	g. threatening
_____	8. obtain	h. small

Answers:

1. e	3. c	5. d	7. h
2. f	4. g	6. a	8. b

Review Letters J-L-M-N-O

Give the word that matches each italicized synonym in the sentences below.

PART A

1. The billowing storm clouds were *threatening*. o_____

2. The senator's *heritage* lives on in his state. l_____

3. Don't *risk* your friendship with Sue by loaning her money.
   j_____

4. With a new political party in office, the differences will *reveal* themselves very quickly. m_____

5. Calvin tends to *misunderstand* my motivations when I explain my political differences to him. m_____

6. The museum *got* the Renoir paintings at a very reasonable price. o_____

7. I am frustrated because my new word processor is *working improperly*. m_____

PART B

1. The city granted a *very profitable* contract to the auto-towing company. l_____

2. Elaine is a perfect bookkeeper because she is *very careful*.
   m_____

3. Admission to the concert was by a *small* donation. n_____

4. Be sure you don't *leave out* the tax when totalling the price of supplies. o_____

5. Louis hopes not to remain an *unknown* poet for long.
   o_____

6. The bad news about layoffs was *lessened* when we heard about the extremely generous severance package.
   m_____

7. The trip to Paris was exciting for Paula, who always complained that her life was *ordinary*. m_____

PART C

1. Without enough people working, the job is *difficult.*
   o_____

2. An increased volume of sales will *offset* the low prices.
   n_____

3. I underestimated the *size* of the problem. m_____

4. Stanley was so opinionated, the rest of the team thought he was trying to *control* them. m_____

5. The couple avoided *public* displays of affection, so as not to make their co-workers uncomfortable. o_____

6. The director of operations was *authorized* to cut costs.
   m_____

Answers

A. 1. ominous   4. manifest   6. obtained
      2. legacy   5. misconstrue   7. malfunctioning
      3. jeopardize

B. 1. lucrative   4. omit   6. mitigated
      2. meticulous   5. obscure   7. mundane
      3. nominal

C. 1. onerous   3. magnitude   5. overt
      2. neutralize   4. manipulate   6. mandated

- P -

paradigm (*paradeigma* pattern G) **model, ideal; example**

The members of the Research & Development Department are **paradigms** of the kind of employees we want to attract to Widget, Inc.

An excellent role model for all, Larry was a **paradigm** of thrift, efficiency, and enthusiasm.

paradox (*para* before + *dokein* to think G) **apparently contradictory, inconsistent; puzzling**

paradoxical

As we consider moving our packaging plant outside of the city, we face a **paradox**; the cost of skilled labor will be cheaper, but skilled labor will be harder to find.

Albert's decision to start his own company struck us as **paradoxical** since he always hoped to become an executive in a Fortune 500 firm.

parameter (*metron* meter G) **limit, boundary, guideline**

"The court has established the **parameters** of the Constitution, and my concern is whether Judge Bork fits within these parameters."
— Sen. Arlen Specter (R–PA), on ABC News' *This Week with David Brinkley*

What is the lower **parameter** for the safety of this product?

perceive (*capere* to take L-F) **see, notice, view**

perceptible
perception
perceptive
imperceptible (ant.)

"I can see a day when pro-choice politics is **perceived** by politicians all over this country as being the safe politics."
— Rep. Les AuCoin (D–OR), on CBS News' *Face The Nation*

If we enlarged the letters, that sign would be **perceptible** from several blocks away.

perfunctory (*fungi* to perform L) **mechanical, superficial, unfeeling**
perfunctorily

Brad's "Good morning" smile seems **perfunctory**.

This survey must have been answered **perfunctorily** by the respondents; the answers show little variation or imagination.

perish (*per* thoroughly, destructively + *ire* to go L-F) **die, expire, pass away**
perishable

Fire drills are meant to ensure that no one would **perish** in a real fire.

Is this product **perishable**, or will it last indefinitely?

perpetuate (*petere* to go L-F) **make (something) last, keep or keep up, preserve**
perpetual
(in) perpetuity

He will **perpetuate** his progressive policies by hiring people who think like him.

The organization's past president, Dr. Johnson, will be remembered in **perpetuity** because of his tremendous leadership.

perplex (*plectere* to braid L) **confuse, puzzle, baffle**
perplexing

The matter of trade and exchange rates and their impact on the world's economies **perplexes** many otherwise well-informed managers.

Esther's decision to reorganize the files was **perplexing** to the secretaries, who found them quite easy to use.

perspective (*pro* forward + *specere* to look L-F) **view, viewpoint, point of view**

As a manager with two hundred people on his staff, Bill's **perspective** was ideal for identifying future managers.

Janet was able to offer a fresh **perspective** on the agricultural equipment account, because she grew up on a farm.

pertain (to) (*tenere* to hold L-F) **have to do with, relate or refer (to)**
pertinent

These issues **pertain** to retirement, so I am referring you to the office that handles those matters.

The staff members were encouraged to discuss only issues **pertinent** to the agenda so that their meeting would end on time.

pervasive (*vadere* to go L) **widespread, extensive**
pervade

"If I were the president, I'd call in the inspector generals from each of the Cabinet agencies and say, I want you to dig into every agency in government to see how **pervasive** this [scandal] is."
— Sen. Robert Dole (R–KS), on CBS News' *Face The Nation*

A sense of excitement **pervades** the office during the week before the holiday vacation.

phenomenon (*phainein* to show G) **event, occurrence, happening**
phenomena (plural)
phenomenal

"If you look back over the history of the situation, the under-evaluation of the marketplace has been there a long time. This isn't a short-term **phenomenon**."
— T. Boone Pickens, Jr., Chairman, Mesa Petroleum, in *Planning Review*

In a **phenomenal** move, Congress overrode the President's veto by a single vote.

platitude (*plat* flat OF) **a dull or trite remark**
To inspire an audience of passive spectators, it takes more than a string of **platitudes**.

The employees heard inspiring comments instead of **platitudes** in the chairman's annual meeting address.

polarize (*polus* pole L-F) **produce or generate two opposing factions, positions, or views**

polarization

> Paula's decision to acquire the financially-troubled firm **polarized** her staff; some felt it was a good turnaround opportunity, while others thought it was a lost cause.

> The research & development and the accounting departments are inevitably in a state of **polarization**; one wants to spend, the other to cut back.

pragmatic (*pragmaticus* skilled in law or business L) **practical, down-to-earth, realistic**

pragmatism

> "You've got to be realistic and **pragmatic** in dealing with the Nicaraguan situation."
> > — Sen. Christopher Dodd (D–CT), on ABC News' *This Week with David Brinkley*

> Heather's **pragmatism** won out, and she convinced us to trim the more costly items from the budget.

precarious (*precarius* obtained by entreaty L) **dangerous, risky, unsafe**

precariously

> "[The debt situation of LDCs] is already **precarious**, but for the moment we are rolling over debt and making concessions."
> > — Henry Kaufman, Partner and Chief Economist, Salomon Brothers Inc., in *Across the Board*

> Although we came **precariously** close to our deadline, the manuscript was delivered to the printer on time.

precipitate (*prae* before + *caput* head L) **cause, bring about, provoke, trigger**

precipitation

> "Although the deficit was not a **precipitating** factor in Friday's [stock market drop], it remains a very serious problem."
> > — Sen. George J. Mitchell, (D–ME), on CBS News' *Face the Nation*

Jane's decision to decorate her office **precipitated** a beautification trend throughout the department.

- QUIZ -

Match the Tier II word in the first column with its synonym in the second column.

_____	1. parameter	a. die
_____	2. perspective	b. widespread
_____	3. perish	c. confuse
_____	4. precarious	d. limit
_____	5. pervasive	e. cause
_____	6. paradoxical	f. event
_____	7. pragmatic	g. mechanical
_____	8. perpetuate	h. viewpoint
_____	9. pertain (to)	i. dangerous
_____	10. perceive	j. puzzling
_____	11. precipitate	k. preserve
_____	12. perplex	l. practical
_____	13. phenomenon	m. relate (to)
_____	14. perfunctory	n. produce opposing sides
_____	15. paradigm	o. dull remark
_____	16. polarize	p. see
_____	17. platitude	q. model

Answers:

1. d	6. j	10. p	14. g
2. h	7. l	11. e	15. q
3. a	8. k	12. c	16. n
4. i	9. m	13. f	17. o
5. b			

preclude (*praecludere* to shut off, close L) **prevent, make impossible**

preclusion
preclusive

Missing the deadline for entries **precludes** our being able to compete in the trophy competition.

Nan's **preclusion** from running again for mayor does not keep her from holding other offices in the town government.

predicate (*praedicare* to assert L) **base, found**

The company **predicated** its sales budget on the assumption that the GNP would not grow in the coming year.

My ability to complete the data entry is **predicated** on there being an available computer.

preeminent (*praeminere* to project forward L) **distinguished, superior, peerless**

preeminence
preeminently

Our goal is to become the **preeminent** computer manufacturer in the world.

The **preeminence** of the Office of the Chairman is such that everyone admires its holder.

preempt (*praeemptus* brought beforehand ML) **seize upon, take the place of, gain an advantage, "beat to the punch" (colloq.)**

preemptor
preemption
preemptive

By making a high and early bid on the manuscript, the publisher sought to **preempt** the competition.

The **preemptive** bid for our competitors' customers proved to be very successful because we obtained several major contracts.

premature (*maturus* ripe L) **too early, too soon**

prematurely

"It might be **premature** to jump from . . . the right of free travel by East Germans all the way over to reunification."
— James A. Baker III, Secretary of State, on CBS News'
Face The Nation

I'm afraid we planned to market our product in Italy **prematurely**; when we realized how high the tariffs would be, we had to reconsider.

premise (*mittere* to send L-F) **assumption**

> "I would reject the **premise** that Congress is tied up in knots."
> — Sen. Sam Nunn (D–GA), on NBC News' *Meet the Press*

Given the **premise** that the company with the lowest manufacturing costs will be most profitable, we proposed building the largest plants in the industry.

prerogative (*rogare* to ask L-F) **right, privilege**

> "It's a **prerogative** of the Ways and Means Committee and the House of Representatives to write the tax law."
> — Rep. Dan Rostenkowski (D–IL), on ABC News' *This Week with David Brinkley*

Although it was the jurors' **prerogative** to disagree with one another, the judge sent them back for more deliberations in hopes of a verdict.

presumptuous (*sumere* to take L) **audacious, arrogant, overstepping bounds**

presume
presumption
presumptive

> "I think it's **presumptuous** for us to assume that we could help the Soviet Union."
> — Sen. Bill Bradley (D–NJ), on CBS News' *Face The Nation*

It was **presumptuous** of me to think that our company would sponsor my softball team when there was no history of such support.

prevail (*valere* to be strong L) **win, succeed, triumph, overcome**

prevailing

> To **prevail** in a more competitive economy, companies must become more receptive to change and become more productive.

Although many people criticize both the Democrats and Republicans, the **prevailing** belief is that one must choose between the two.

prevalent (*valere* to be strong L) **common, widespread, customary, current**

prevalence

> Frequent job changes are becoming **prevalent** in Japan, where once they were very unusual.

> The weakness of the economic recovery is indicated by the **prevalence** of high unemployment.

problematic(al) (*pro* before + *ballein* to throw G) **doubtful, uncertain, unsettled, indefinite; difficult to solve**

> The outcome of the negotiations with our largest customer is so **problematic**, it is not worth speculating about.

> The decision to build a new plant is **problematic** because prices are falling and competition has announced new capacity expansions.

prodigious (*agere* to drive L) **huge, enormous, tremendous, wondrous**

prodigy

> Mary must have **prodigious** mathematical skills to have been able to write that analysis of pricing theory.

> Gary is something of a **prodigy**; at 22 years of age, he is our youngest chairman of the board ever.

profound (*fundus* bottom L) **deep, deeply felt**

profoundly
profundity

> "The first effect [of a crash] on a given airline is a very **profound** disappointment and a terrible shock that goes through the whole organization."
>   — Robert L. Crandell, Chairman, President and CEO, American Airlines, Inc., on ABC News' *This Week with David Brinkley*

> Larry was **profoundly** touched by the get-well-soon cards that we sent him when he was out with the flu.

proliferate (*proles* progeny + *fere* yielding L-F) **spread or grow quickly, multiply**

proliferation

Use of personal computers has **proliferated** throughout our company.

The **proliferation** of flower shops on Broadway has brought the price of roses down considerably.

propensity (*pendere* to hang L) **tendency, inclination**

"Along with his political philosophy or ideology, you have to consider [Judge Bork's] **propensity** for activism."
— Sen. Howell Heflin (D–AL), on ABC News' *This Week with David Brinkley*

His **propensity** for lateness marred his otherwise excellent work record.

proprietary (*proprius* own L) **privately owned, exclusive**

"With Microsoft, a lot of questions existed about whether IBM was going to go **proprietary**, close down the interface, and not support third party software."
— William C. Lowe, President, Entry Systems Division, IBM Corp., in *PC World*

She wanted **proprietary** rights for the trademarks, but her lawyer told her she was too late: the rights had already been granted to another party.

provincialism (*provincia* province + *alis* pertaining to L) **narrowness of mind, ignorance**

provincial
provincially

Since he came from a small business, Jim's **provincialism** initially prevented him from feeling comfortable in the culture of the multinational firm.

At first, Joan's **provincial** background kept her from appreciating the many cultural attractions of the city.

prudent (*videre* to see L-F) **wise, sensible, careful**

imprudent (ant.)
prudence
prudently

"Success is the carrot—the reward of competence and hard work and diligence, and **prudent** management."
— Sen. William Proxmire (D–WI), in *The New York Times*

The mutual fund lost much of its value because of Ralph's **imprudent** management.

- Q -

qualitative (*qualis* of what kind L-F) **relating to qualities or traits rather than quantity**

"I have also thought it important to put in writing these **qualitative** aspects of business which we have called 'corporate purpose.'"
— Geoffrey Simmonds, Chairman, Hercules Aerospace Co., in *Across the Board*

We don't have the data to give a quantitative presentation, but we can discuss it **qualitatively**.

- QUIZ -

Match the Tier II word in the first column with its synonym in the second column.

_____	1. prevail	a. distinguished
_____	2. prerogative	b. too early
_____	3. propensity	c. spread quickly
_____	4. preeminent	d. win
_____	5. predicate	e. involving traits
_____	6. problematic	f. privilege
_____	7. prevalent	g. privately owned
_____	8. provincialism	h. tendency
_____	9. premature	i. base
_____	10. proliferate	j. uncertain
_____	11. profound	k. enormous
_____	12. premise	l. audacious
_____	13. prudent	m. assumption
_____	14. prodigious	n. seize upon
_____	15. presumptuous	o. deep
_____	16. proprietary	p. wise
_____	17. preclude	q. narrow view
_____	18. preempt	r. common
_____	19. qualitative	s. prevent

Answers:

1. d	6. j	11. o	16. g
2. f	7. r	12. m	17. s
3. h	8. q	13. p	18. n
4. a	9. b	14. k	19. e
5. i	10. c	15. l	

Review Letter P-Q

Which word most closely suits the italicized definition in the sentences below?

PART A

1. Eve had a unique *point of view* on the project. p_____
2. We feared the flu would *spread quickly* because few of the staff had been vaccinated. p_____
3. Our company has an *exclusive* technology to manufacture the new drug. p_____
4. The equinox is a twice-a-year *occurrence*. p_____
5. Did you *notice* the subtle differences in the faked painting? p_____
6. I am operating under the *assumption* that the economy is improving. p_____
7. Imagine our surprise when we found we'd been *beaten to the punch* before we even placed our bid. p_____
8. The new chairman has pledged to *preserve* our commitment to a clean environment. p_____
9. It was *too early* to start hiring people because the company wasn't profitable yet. p_____
10. The mayor kept repeating the same *dull remark*, and she lost the audience's interest. p_____
11. Heather was *realistic* about our potential for expansion. p_____
12. Confidence in the automobile industry is less *widespread* than it once was. p_____

PART B

1. To lower-income families, the effect of a tax levy would be *deeply* felt. p_____
2. I'm looking forward to hearing a speech by the *distinguished* scientist. p_____

3. Mr. Linden's toy company was in a *risky* position for some time, but now it is thriving. p_____

4. My introduction of the speaker was *superficial*, because I didn't have a chance to learn more about her before the conference. p_____

5. It would be *wise* to watch the photocopier being fixed before trying to fix it yourself. p_____

6. Whether the trade agreement will be good for small business is *doubtful*, and the experts are divided on the issue. p_____

7. Caesar's behavior was intended to *baffle* me—and ensured the surprise party was a success. p_____

8. It was *audacious* of Tim to think that he would be promoted so soon. p_____

9. Ned's plans for the advertising campaign might *prevent* my suggestions from being used. p_____

10. The controversy over pension benefits will *produce opposing views between* management and labor. p_____

11. The question of interest rates *has to do with* the banking industry. p_____ (to)

12. A problem of petty pilfering *is spread throughout* the industry. p_____

PART C
1. The veto is the President's *privilege*. p_____

2. Finding the missing contact lens will take a *tremendous* effort. p_____

3. The need to produce more goods before we hire any additional staff seems like a *contradiction*. p_____

4. Many economists believe that high interest rates will *bring about* a recession. p_____

5. Once a frequent gambler, Kelly realized that hard work would *triumph* over luck. p_____

6. Two coal miners *died* in the explosion. p_____

7. Mrs. Blum has a *tendency* toward correcting everyone's grammar. p_____

8. Our success is *based* on a philosophy of old-fashioned service.
   p_____

9. The firm's *narrowness of mind* kept it from expanding into computers while it still had a chance. p_____

10. Joe produced both a numerical and a *trait-oriented* analysis of the population. q_____

11. One hopes for a president who will be an *example* of greatness.
    (a) p_____

12. We must set *limits* for the investigation and see that it fits within our budget. p_____

Answers

A.
1. perspective	5. perceive	9. premature
2. proliferate	6. premise	10. platitude
3. proprietary	7. preempted	11. pragmatic
4. phenomenon	8. perpetuate	12. prevalent

B.
1. profoundly	5. prudent	9. preclude
2. preeminent	6. problematic	10. polarize
3. precarious	7. perplex	11. pertains (to)
4. perfunctory	8. presumptuous	12. pervades

C.
1. prerogative	5. prevail	9. provincialism
2. prodigious	6. perished	10. qualitative
3. paradox	7. propensity	11. paradigm
4. precipitate	8. predicated	12. parameters

- R -

ramification (*ramus* branch L-F) **result, effect, consequence**

"All **ramifications** of the new [manufacturing] plant on the business will be factored into the analysis."
> — Paul E. Lego, President and COO, Westinghouse Electric Corp., in *Planning Review*

The arrival of lower interest rates has many **ramifications** for lenders and borrowers alike.

reciprocate (*reciprocus* alternating L) **return the favor, pay back, respond in kind**

reciprocal
reciprocity

We did the company a favor, and it has **reciprocated** by starting to buy from us.

Under our **reciprocal** agreement with XYZ Computers, their staff trains our technical support force, and we repair their hardware at a discount rate.

reconciliation (*re* back, again + *conciliare* to assemble L) **settlement, making or patching up**

reconcile
reconcilable
reconciliatory
irreconcilable (ant.)

Many promising **reconciliations** have broken down because while both parties came prepared to forgive, neither party came prepared to be forgiven.
> — Charles Williams, Episcopal bishop, 1860–1923

The company's president met with union officials to **reconcile** the gap between the union's request for a 10 percent raise and management's offer of 6 percent.

rectify (*rectus* right L-F) **fix, correct, set right**

rectifiable
rectification

> Army: A body of men assembled to **rectify** the mistakes of the diplomats.
> — Josephus Daniel, statesman, 1862–1948

> The pollution violations were not **rectifiable** within 90 days, so ABC Steel paid a large fine.

refrain (*frangere* to break L-F) **hold back or keep oneself from doing something, stop**

> Monkeys very sensibly **refrain** from speech, lest they should be set to earn their livings.
> — Anonymous

> Management was reminded to **refrain** from discussing the buyout because of S.E.C. regulations.

refute (*futare* to beat L) **disprove, deny**

irrefutable (ant.)
refutable
refutation

> Who can **refute** a sneer?
> — William Paley, English philosopher, 1743–1805

> The charges in the trial had been so carefully worded that they were **irrefutable**.

reiterate (*iterum* again L) **repeat, restate**

> Let me **reiterate**, we cannot accept return merchandise when the package has been opened.

> He **reiterated** the statement he'd made six months earlier: he would not run for a third term.

relegate (*legare* to send as emissary L) **assign to an inferior position, transfer**

> Herbert was a vice president of finance, but due to a major fiasco in the department he has been **relegated** to a minor position on the finance staff.

The projected plans for expansion were **relegated** to the back burner while the company's finances were examined very carefully.

relentless (*lentus* tough, slow L) **unbending, merciless, strict**
relentlessly
relentlessness

Jon was **relentless** in repeating his budget-cutting message, and soon the words began to sink in.

The waves pounded the beach **relentlessly** during the hurricane.

relinquish (*linguire* to leave L-F) **give up, let go (of), yield**

The successful businessman **relinquishes** bad habits and replaces them with good ones.

Mediocre T.V. shows caused the network to **relinquish** first place and take a smaller share of the market.

reminiscent (*reminisci* to remember L) **relating to a remembered experience; tending to remind or recall; suggestive**
reminisce
reminiscence

The breaking up of AT&T is **reminiscent** in some ways of trustbusting in the early twentieth century.

Longtime employees enjoyed **reminiscing** about the early days of the company.

repercussions (*repercussion* rebounding L) **an effect which is often remote, indirect, or long-term**

The **repercussions** of the company's first failure to pay a yearly dividend were felt throughout the industry.

The Sputnik space program had both short term effects, such as, the race to the moon and long term **repercussions**, such as, the exploration of space.

replenish (*plein* full L-F) **refill, restock, resupply**
replenishment

Could you **replenish** our stock of computer disks?

Our office supplies need **replenishment** on a weekly basis; otherwise we run out.

reprehensible (*prehendere* to grasp L) **blameworthy, condemnable, shameful, disgraceful**

John's illegal borrowing of $1,000 from the company's Christmas Toys For Tots Fund was **reprehensible**.

The case of sexual harassment was especially **reprehensible** because the individual charged is the manager of the Human Resources Department.

- QUIZ -

Match the Tier II word in the first column with its synonym in the second column.

_____ 1. rectify	a. disprove
_____ 2. refute	b. assign
_____ 3. reconciliation	c. repeat
_____ 4. reminiscent	d. refill
_____ 5. refrain	e. settlement
_____ 6. relegate	f. give up
_____ 7. reciprocate	g. disgraceful
_____ 8. relinquish	h. consequence
_____ 9. reiterate	i. fix
_____ 10. replenish	j. pay back
_____ 11. ramification	k. hold back
_____ 12. reprehensible	l. suggestive
_____ 13. repercussions	m. merciless
_____ 14. relentless	n. indirect effects

Answers:

1. i	5. k	9. c	13. n
2. a	6. b	10. d	14. m
3. e	7. j	11. h	
4. l	8. f	12. g	

reprimand (*reprimere* to check L-F) **rebuke, censure, criticize**

Juanita sharply **reprimanded** Sue for not attending the meeting.

The congressman **reprimanded** his staff for the faulty way the press conference was handled.

repudiate (*repudium* divorce L) **reject, disown, disclaim, cast off**
repudiation

One would hope that any candidate for office would **repudiate** the support of known racists.

Jill's chances for reelection were doomed after her **repudiation** by the voters in the primary.

resilient (*salire* to leap L) **elastic, buoyant, flexible, able to bounce back**
resilience

"This is a **resilient** society."
— Lee A. Iacocca, Chairman and CEO, Chrysler Corp., in *Quality Progress*

To succeed, a person needs to show **resilience** in the face of disappointment.

resolute (*resolvere* to unfasten, loosen L) **firm, steadfast, fixed**
resolution

The department chair was **resolute** in her decision to step down, despite many appeals to her to stay.

After his first defeat, the governor made a firm **resolution** to work toward being reelected.

respond (*spondere* to promise L-F) **answer, reply; react**
respondent
response
responsive

If you can't **respond** to a man's arguments, all is not lost; you can still call him vile names.
— Elbert Hubbard, American author, 1856–1915

The company built a loyal customer base because of its reputation as being highly **responsive** to customer needs.

restore   (*restaurare* to renew L-F)   **give back, return; bring back, repair**

restoration

> "We came forward with an alternative [tax] which would have **restored** individual retirement accounts for first home purchase, for college education and for retirement."
> — Rep. Thomas S. Foley (D–WA), on NBC News' *Meet The Press*

The **restoration** of the drug company's reputation was never in doubt as they responded quickly and thoroughly to the stories of drug poisoning.

retain   (*tenere* to hold L-F)   **keep, hold, save**

retention

> The sum of behavior is to **retain** a man's own dignity, without intruding upon the liberty of others.
> — Francis Bacon

Retention of the profit-sharing provision in the retirement plan has made the company very popular among workers in the industry.

retaliate   (*talio* legal retaliation L)   **get back, get even, pay back**

retaliation
retaliatory

> The competition has taken our largest customer and we have to **retaliate** immediately.

The aggressive moves of the computer corporation met **retaliation** from Widget Computers, which responded with another round of price cuts.

reticence   (*tacere* to be silent L)   **state of being reserved, restrained, or uncommunicative**

reticent

> While everyone else spoke in favor of the proposal, Jerry's **reticence** was taken to signify disapproval.

Because of her shyness, Jill was **reticent** when asked to tell the group something about herself.

(in) retrospect (*retro* back + *specere* to look L) **on reflection, looking back, on second thought**
retrospective

In **retrospect**, we should have taken less risk and built a smaller plant because there was too much uncertainty in this business.

A **retrospective** of the company's first ten years shows a steady growth of profits.

revert (*vertere* to turn L-F) **return, change or turn back, regress**
reversion

The salesmen are much less motivated under the new sales compensation program; we should **revert** to our previous system of payment by commission only.

The clause calling for **reversion** of profits to the original owner will be changed so that profits go to the buyer instead.

revise (*videre* to see L-F) **change, amend, correct**
revision
unrevised (ant.)

We need to **revise** our financial and accounting procedures if we are to stay up-to-date.

The schools had to continue to use the old edition of the text when its **revision** was postponed by the publisher.

rhetoric (*rhetor* orator G-F) **high-flown language; sometimes insincere eloquence**
rhetorical

"I believe [presidential comments regarding the space program] are only **rhetoric** until such time as the President shows us where the money's coming from."
— Sen. Sam Nunn (D–GA), on NBC News' *Meet The Press*

As a speaker, she uses, fine, **rhetorical** prose; the problem is that her solutions seldom match the fancy prose that describes them.

rivalry (*rivalis* one using the same stream as another L-F)
opposition, competition

rival
unrivaled (ant.)

> "I think [President Ortega's threat to end the ceasefire] grows
> out of a **rivalry** that he feels toward President Arias of Costa
> Rica, who hosted the meeting there."
> — Sen. George J. Mitchell (D–ME), on NBC News' *Meet
> The Press*

As **rivals** for the presidency, both women knew that only one
of them could win.

- QUIZ -

Match the Tier II word in the first column with its synonym or definition in the second column.

_____	1. resilient	a. looking back
_____	2. retain	b. opposition
_____	3. revise	c. keep
_____	4. reprimand	d. bring back
_____	5. revert	e. disown
_____	6. rivalry	f. get even
_____	7. rhetoric	g. rebuke
_____	8. restore	h. change back
_____	9. repudiate	i. reserved
_____	10. retaliate	j. able to bounce back
_____	11. (in) retrospect	k. change
_____	12. reticent	l. firm
_____	13. resolute	m. answer
_____	14. respond	n. high-flown language

Answers:

1. j	5. h	9. e	13. l
2. c	6. b	10. f	14. m
3. k	7. n	11. a	
4. g	8. d	12. i	

Review Letter R

Fill in the Tier II words that are synonymous with the italicized words in the following sentences.

PART A

1. After exercising daily for six months, Bob was ready to *go back* to his old sedentary ways. r_____

2. I will now *repeat* the fire drill instructions. r_____

3. Leonard is trying to *bring back* the wonderful reputation his restaurant had in the past. r_____

4. What will be the short-term *consequences* of our changing the company name? r_____

5. Reducing the size of the country's military should *fix* the budget imbalance. r_____

6. Don't *criticize* her; she is just following incorrect instructions. r_____

7. The long-term *effects* of today's cost-cutting measures will come back to haunt us. r_____

8. Jim's *reserve* at the contract negotiation was taken as tacit acceptance. r_____

9. Please *reply* quickly to my request for information. r_____

PART B

1. It's a good idea to *save* your receipt until you're sure the product works. r_____

2. There is a healthy *competition* between the two top copywriters in the marketing department. r_____

3. Because Amy was *able to bounce back* after a loss, she was an ideal candidate for the team. r_____

4. Tina will *change* the agenda to reflect new concerns. r_____

5. The heavy rains should *refill* the reservoirs. r_____

6. Carolyn tried to *hold back* from coughing during the concert.
    r_____

7. The board of directors agreed to *give up* its control of the situation and let the company president take over.
    r_____

8. The candidate was *merciless* in her attacks on her opponent.
    r_____

9. She is *steadfast* in her decision to move to a warmer climate.
    r_____

PART C

1. We should *return the favor* by inviting them to dine at our house. r_____

2. Ray easily *disproved* the allegations against him. r_____

3. I am tempted to *get even* for the unfair treatment I received.
    r_____

4. Wilma still hopes to see things *patched up* with her partners.
    r_____

5. In *looking back*, everything seems clear. r_____

6. The comptroller *disclaimed* any allegations of his responsibility for the fiscal crisis. r_____

7. Nancy has been *assigned* to the back office because of her errors. r_____

8. Jeremiah's behavior is *shameful.* r_____

9. The speaker's *high-flown language* alienated his listeners.
    r_____

10. Bell bottom pants are *a reminder* of the 1960s. r_____

Answers

A. 1. revert
2. reiterate
3. restore

4. ramifications
5. rectify
6. reprimand

7. repercussions
8. reticence
9. respond

B. 1. retain
2. rivalry
3. resilient

4. revise
5. replenish
6. refrain

7. relinquish
8. relentless
9. resolute

C. 1. reciprocate
2. refuted
3. retaliate
4. reconciled

5. retrospect
6. repudiated
7. relegated

8. reprehensible
9. rhetoric
10. reminiscent

- S -

sacrifice (*sacer* holy + *facere* to make L-F) **give or offer up, forfeit**
sacrificial

> Self-sacrifice enables us to **sacrifice** other people without blushing.
> — George Bernard Shaw

> The staff had no desire to be **sacrificial** lambs on the altar of company economizing.

sanction (*sancire* to make holy L-F) **approve, authorize, permit**

> The executive board has **sanctioned** our decision to acquire the insurance company.

> Travel expenses are **sanctioned** by the company with some restrictions: for example, one may only fly economy class.

sanguine (*sanguis* blood L-F) **hopeful, optimistic; cheerful**

> The encouraging news about the deficit will make most economists **sanguine** about an improvement in the economy.

> The mayor is **sanguine** that, with tax breaks, Widget, Inc. will be persuaded to keep its headquarters in New York.

scrutinize (*scrutari* to search fr. *scruta* trash L) **look carefully at, examine, inspect, "eyeball"**
scrutiny

> Not all things have to be **scrutinized**, nor all friends tested, nor all enemies exposed and denounced.
> — Anonymous

> All candidates must undergo the **scrutiny** of a committee of recruiters.

sentiment (*sentire* to perceive L) **feeling, opinion; emotion**
sentimental

> The **sentiment** on the budget committee is to eliminate salary increases during the recession.

The citizens voiced their **sentiment** when they voted for the tax increase in order to pay for health care.

skeptical (*skeptesthai* to look, consider G) **doubtful, mistrustful, suspicious**

skeptic
skepticism

"I was very **skeptical** about any diversification."
— Thomas Watson, Chairman, IBM Corp., in *The Wall Street Journal*

Others may believe in the prospect of a national system of health care in the United States, but Terry is a **skeptic**.

solicit (*sollicitare* to disturb L-F) **ask or ask for, request, invite**

solicitation
solicitor
unsolicited (ant.)

"I don't want to give **unsolicited** advice; I can only talk about my experience at Ford."
— Philip Caldwell, Chairman, Ford Motor Co., in *The New York Times*

Some residential neighborhoods forbid the door-to-door **solicitation** of business.

spectrum (*specere* to look L) **range, extent**

"We've begun to question our entire system, our entire manufacturing processes right across the **spectrum** [of products]."
— Anthony J. F. Reilly, CEO, H. J. Heinz Co., in *Fortune*

The wide **spectrum** of investment choices can be both exciting and intimidating to the new investor.

speculate (*speculari* to spy out fr. *specere* to look L) **guess, imagine**

speculation
speculative
speculator

"I won't **speculate** on what graphic standard we will support in our new operating systems offerings."

— William C. Lowe, President, Energy Systems Division, IBM Corp., in *PC World*

When the vice-president resigned from the company, there was much **speculation** on who would be appointed as the next vice-president.

- QUIZ -

Match the Tier II word in the first column with its synonym in the second column.

_____	1. sanguine	a. feeling
_____	2. sentiment	b. permit
_____	3. sanction	c. guess
_____	4. spectrum	d. give up
_____	5. scrutinize	e. doubtful
_____	6. speculate	f. examine
_____	7. sacrifice	g. range
_____	8. solicit	h. hopeful
_____	9. skeptical	i. ask for

Answers:

1. h	4. g	6. c	8. i
2. a	5. f	7. d	9. e
3. b			

---

stigmatize (*stizein* to tattoo G) **mark, brand, or label negatively**

stigma

Our industry has been wrongly **stigmatized** as irresponsible about environmental issues.

Many innocent brokers who sold junk bonds now bear a **stigma** because of the criminal actions of a few.

subordinate (*sub* under + *ordon* rank, order L) **place in a lower order or rank; reduce**

subordination

> Because of the crisis, it was necessary to **subordinate** key long-term programs to short-term programs which would control the crisis.

> After being in charge of her own unit, Janice was not used to being in a state of **subordination** to others.

substantiate (*stare* to stand L-F) **prove, confirm, verify**

substantiation

> "I have no grounds, based on my observation during the four-and-one-half-hour meeting, to **substantiate** that [Gorbachev was under internal pressure not to visit the U.S.]."
> — Frank Carlucci, Secretary of Defense, on ABC News' *This Week with David Brinkley*

> The reporter checked her facts carefully in order to provide **substantiation** for the rumor that the company was going public.

substantive (*stare* to stand L-F) **real, actual; important**

substantial
insubstantial (ant.)

> "When you talk about **substantive** issues, there are only two presidents who were going to repeal Warren's decisions by putting different kinds of judges on the Supreme Court."
> — Sen. Birch Bayh (D–IN), on ABC News' *This Week with David Brinkley*

> The union was insisting on a **substantial** increase in wages, despite management's offer of a more modest raise.

superficial (*superficies* top, surface L-F) **shallow, surface; not thorough, cursory; petty**

superficially
superficiality

> In the interest of time, we first conducted a **superficial** study on our transportation problems, with a more thorough study to follow.

The auditors only glanced **superficially** through the company's financial records instead of making a detailed examination.

supersede (*super* over + *sedere* to sit L-F) **replace, supplant**

I understand a new EPA document will **supersede** the current regulations.

The hardcharging vice president was **superseded** by a soft-spoken, but extremely effective new person.

suppress (*premere* to press L) **hide, conceal, keep secret**

suppression

We need to **suppress** the news about our planned acquisition in order to prevent insider trading.

The **suppression** of all news of the uprising was achieved by imposing a blackout on the press.

surreptitious (*rapere* to seize L) **secret, covert, sneaky**

surreptitiously

There is no question that he got the information on our competitor's sales **surreptitiously**.

The **surreptitious** gathering of information about a company's competition is more common than one might think.

sustain (*tenere* to hold L-F) **maintain, support**

sustainable
sustenance

"We have to be careful that the [budget] cuts are real, that they are **sustainable** from year to year."
— Rep. Thomas Foley (D–WA), on ABC News' *This Week with David Brinkley*

It is a challenge to the Federal Reserve to **sustain** steady economic growth without triggering inflation.

synergy (*syn* together + *ergon* work G) **combined or cooperative action**

synergism
synergistic

"The rationale we came up with was that the acquisition would fit into our consumer products group and was **synergistic** with our Sunday School book publishing company."
— Robert E. Weissman, President and COO, The Dun & Bradstreet Corp., in *Planning Review*

The **synergism** between the newly united companies was so successful that their combined earnings in the first year of the joint venture were 20 percent greater than their separate earnings the previous year.

synthesis (*syn* + *tithenai* to put G) **combination, fusion, blend**
synthesize

Napoleon, the **synthesis** of brute and Superman.
— Friederich Nietzsche

The publisher's goal was to **synthesize** the goals of his sales and editorial departments rather than to keep them separate.

systemic (*histanai* to cause to stand G) **of or relating to an (entire) system**

"Once we get through these two days, we will know whether there has been any real **systemic** damage done or not [as a result of the October stock market crash]."
— John Phelan, Chairman, New York Stock Exchange, on ABC News' *This Week with David Brinkley*

A decision to impose price controls on drugs might have a **systemic** impact on the entire pharmaceutical industry.

- QUIZ -

Match the Tier II word in the first column with its synonym in the second column.

_____	1. superficial	a. reduce in rank
_____	2. stigmatize	b. prove
_____	3. synergistic	c. secretly
_____	4. systemic	d. real
_____	5. synthesis	e. shallow
_____	6. supersede	f. maintainable
_____	7. substantive	g. brand
_____	8. surreptitiously	h. relating to a system
_____	9. sustainable	i. hide
_____	10. substantiate	j. blend
_____	11. suppress	k. replace
_____	12. subordinate	l. productively interactive

Answers:

1. e	4. h	7. d	10. b
2. g	5. j	8. c	11. i
3. l	6. k	9. f	12. a

Review Letter S

Write each Tier II word next to the sentence containing the italicized synonym.

PART A

1. The student was *labeled* as a plagiarist because he lifted quotes from others without giving credit.
   s_____

2. The company agreed to *support* the employees' benefits for another year. s_____

3. A more sophisticated computer will *replace* the one you are using now. s_____

4. Because Allen wants the input, he will *invite* your opinions on the factory construction. s_____

5. The general *feeling* in the company was that it should wait until things settle down before investing in Russia.
   s_____

6. We can only *guess* about the election outcome. s_____

7. I can't *approve* any additional spending. s_____

PART B

1. The division must show *real* results in the first quarter.
   s_____

2. Ken admitted the clean-up was *not thorough*. s_____

3. Congress agreed to *reduce* its activities in international problems until domestic issues are solved.
   s_____

4. Ruth seems more *hopeful* about her future now that she has been promoted. s_____

5. Paul is always *mistrustful* of new policies. s_____

6. *Examine* the new brochure to see that there are no errors.
   s_____

7. The report will *confirm* Sharon's beliefs about the project.
   s_____

PART C

1. Be careful to look at the whole *range* of opportunities before investing. s_____

2. The government tried to *hide* the news of the scandal. s_____

3. Their strategy represents a *combination* of many ideas. s_____

4. The movie star's travel arrangements were made *secretly*. s_____

5. Donald *gave up* the opportunity to play golf in order to stay home with his kids. s_____

6. The interruption in telephone service due to sunspots is *system-wide*. s_____

7. Because of *the combined effort* of the task force, it finished the project in record time. s_____

Answers

A. 1. stigmatized   4. solicit   6. speculate
    2. sustain   5. sentiment   7. sanction
    3. supersede

B. 1. substantive   4. sanguine   6. scrutinize
    2. superficial   5. skeptical   7. substantiate
    3. subordinate

C. 1. spectrum   4. surreptitiously   6. systemic
    2. suppress   5. sacrificed   7. synergy
    3. synthesis

- T -

tangential (*tangere* to touch L) **incidental, unrelated, peripheral**
tangent

> "They're really rather **tangential** arguments; they're not
> dealing with the substance of it [Lithuania's declaration of
> independence]."
> — Sen. George J. Mitchell (D–ME), on CBS News' *Face The
> Nation*

Jane found it difficult to stick to the topic in her talk and kept
going off on **tangents**.

tantamount (*tant amunter* to amount to as much AF) **equal,
equivalent, nearly identical**

> Their explanation was **tantamount** to an admission that there
> were quality control problems with the raw materials they
> sent us.

> The union's refusal to consider the company's offer was
> **tantamount** to a breakdown in negotiations.

tarnish (*ternir* to tarnish MF) **stain, dirty, blacken, dishonor**
> The scandal **tarnished** Wall Street's reputation.

> The numerous mistakes in their presentation **tarnished** their
> image of reliability.

tenable (*tenere* to hold L-F) **defensible, supportable, maintainable**
untenable (ant.)

> The company has a highly **tenable** market position due to
> their many patents.

> On the face of all the evidence against them, their defense in
> the trial became more and more **untenable**.

tenuous (*tenuis* thin L) **flimsy, weak**
tenuously

"Every time something about the War Powers Act comes up, we say it is too **tenuous** a situation here . . . but now the [Persian Gulf situation] is the time [to invoke the Act]."
— Sen. John Glenn (D–OH), on ABC News' *This Week with David Brinkley*

With several competing stores now operating in its neighborhood, the fruit and vegetable market is clinging **tenuously** to its hope for survival.

terminate (*terminus* end L-F) **stop, end, conclude**

interminable (ant.)
termination

"My impression is that, even if the Sandinistas were to totally **terminate** their supply of arms to the guerrillas in El Salvador, the war in that country would continue."
— Rep. Stephen Solarz (D–NY), on CBS News' *Face The Nation*

The **termination** of the contract will allow us to negotiate a more favorable arrangement with another vendor.

tolerate (*tolerare* to put up with L) **put up with, stand, bear**

tolerable
tolerance
tolerant
toleration

The business manager would not **tolerate** any opposition to his program.

Sandy thought the wages on her job were good, but the working conditions were barely **tolerable**.

transaction (*trans* across + *agere* to drive L) **deal, (business) agreement**

transact

"Exactly, arms-for-hostages **transactions**."
— Sen. Warren Rudman (R–NH), on ABC News' *This Week with David Brinkley*

Some businessmen prefer to **transact** business on the golf course rather than in an office.

transcend (*scandere* to climb L) **go beyond, exceed, surpass**
transcendence

> The tremendous growth of the new computer company **transcended** the founders' wildest dreams.

> Our business is worldwide, consequently, our politics and loyalties **transcend** national boundaries.

transition (*ire* to go L) **change, shift, (period of) movement**
transitional

> "I had promised the CEO an orderly **transition** [in leadership]."
> > — Robert E. Weissman, President and COO, The Dun & Bradstreet Corp., in *Planning Review*

> ABC Widget Co. faced many **transitional** problems as it was quickly transformed from a local to a national operation.

transmit (*mittere* to send L) **send, convey**
transmission
transmittal

> They **transmitted** the data while we were out of the office.

> The Information Age is dependent on the instantaneous **transmission** of enormous amounts of data around the world.

turmoil (*tur(n)* + *molliare* to make soft L) **great confusion, chaos, disorder, hassle**

> The war in the oil-rich Middle East caused **turmoil** with respect to oil supply and prices.

> Instead of the hoped-for solution to the problem, the mix of conflicting economic advice from all schools-of-thought created **turmoil**.

- QUIZ -

Match the Tier II word in the first column with its synonym in the second column.

_____	1. tarnish	a.	incidental
_____	2. transmit	b.	deal
_____	3. tolerate	c.	go beyond
_____	4. tangential	d.	defensible
_____	5. turmoil	e.	send
_____	6. tantamount	f.	dirty
_____	7. transaction	g.	put up with
_____	8. terminate	h.	hassle
_____	9. transition	i.	weak
_____	10. tenable	j.	change
_____	11. transcend	k.	equal
_____	12. tenuous	l.	stop

Answers:

1. f	4. a	7. b	10. d
2. e	5. h	8. l	11. c
3. g	6. k	9. j	12. i

- U -

unequivocal (*un* not + *aequi* equal + *vox* voice L) **clear, definite, unqualified**

unequivocally

Rick was **unequivocal** in his acceptance of the promotion even though he would have to move from California.

The National Labor Relations Board stated **unequivocally** that a mediator would be sought to end the deadlock between management and union leaders.

unilateral (*unis* one + *lateralis* of the side L) **relating to one side only; not mutual**

unilaterally

> " . . . you can't **unilaterally** cancel weapons systems and encourage arms control agreements."
>> — Rep. Les Aspin (D–WI), on ABC News' *This Week With David Brinkley*

June took full responsibility for her **unilateral** decision that all department heads would only get a one percent raise.

unprecedented (*prae* before + *cedere* to go L-F) **unheard-of, novel, new**

precedent

> "I've got to stress that this is an **unprecedented** situation!"
>> — Rep. Pat Swindall (R–GA), on ABC News' *This Week with David Brinkley*

Gross sales of new books have risen 16 percent to a figure that was **unprecedented** in this publishing house.

unsubstantiated (*sub* under + *stare* to stand L-F) **unproven, unconfirmed, unverified**

The statement that unemployment is growing is **unsubstantiated** in the latest figures from Washington.

The allegations that the controller borrowed funds for his personal use were **unsubstantiated**.

usurp (*usus* use + *rapere* to seize L-F) **wrongfully seize, take, grab**

usurpation

The financial staff has **usurped** control of decisions that used to be made by the production people.

The **usurpation** of traditional department store markets by discount stores has greatly changed consumer spending habits.

- V -

vacillate (*vacillare* to sway L) **change one's mind, be indecisive, hesitate, waver**

vacillation

> Jeff, in your presentation to the company president, don't **vacillate** when answering his questions.

> A successful executive cannot **vacillate**; he must have a firm plan in mind and must act on it without hesitation.

validate (*valere* to be strong L-F) **confirm, formally approve**

valid
validation
validity

> "What we both wanted to do was to **validate** our view by bringing together a team of senior management from our pharmaceutical divisions."
> — Henry Wendt, Chairman, President and CEO,
> SmithKline Beckman Corp., in *The New York Times*

> A state court found that the contract was **valid** and must be honored.

versatile (*vertere* to turn L-F) **well-rounded, generally capable**

versatility

> To become president of this company one must be **versatile** with strengths in engineering, marketing and finance.

> **Versatility** is the key to success in any business: a leader wears many hats.

viable (*vita* life L-F) **capable of living; feasible, workable**

viability

> "[Competition in large volume markets and obligation to serve third world regions with satellite communications] will prevent Intelstat from being an economical, **viable** organization."
> — Irving Goldstein, CEO, Comsat, in *Across the Board*

The **viability** of the new company will depend on the market need for the product and the company's skills in manufacturing it.

vicarious (*vicarius* substituting L) **performed in place of another; felt through others**

vicariously

The retired executive **vicariously** enjoyed seeing his daughter rise through the ranks of the corporation.

Although she was home sick in bed, Eunice **vicariously** enjoyed seeing her colleagues receive their awards on TV.

vindicate (*vindex* avenger L) **set right, clear, excuse**

vindication

"I think [Judge Bork] will have a chance to publicly **vindicate** himself."
— Sen. Birch Bayh (D–IN), on ABC News' *This Week with David Brinkley*

Accused of theft, the bookkeeper sought **vindication** by demanding an audit.

violate (*violare* to violate L) **break, breach**

violation

The supplier **violated** the contract when he missed a delivery because of unexpected plant problems.

The manufacturer charged the buyer with contract **violation** for finding another, cheaper source for the product.

visceral (*viscera* internal organs L) **instinctive; crude**

viscerally

Instead of coolly considering the consequences, Julia's response to the new employee was **visceral** and hostile.

Paul **viscerally** opposed the new product idea rather than thoughtfully considering the matter.

vociferous (*vox* voice + *ferre* to bear L) **loud, noisy, insistent**

vociferously

In contrast to Eric who was supportive but subdued, Alexis was **vociferous** in her support for expansion of the computer staff.

Japan **vociferously** argues that it is the American system that needs overhauling, and not Japan's method of doing business.

volatile (*volare* to fly L-F) **changeable, unstable; explosive**
volatility

"Markets in this country and around the world are becoming much more **volatile** and sensitive to domestic and international news."
— John Phelan, Chairman, New York Stock Exchange, on ABC News' *This Week with David Brinkley*

Politically, the **volatility** of the situation meant that at any moment the government might topple.

vulnerable (*vulnerare* to wound L) **open (to attack), weak, defenseless, exposed**
invulnerability (ant.)
invulnerable (ant.)
vulnerability

"I think our going after Gulf clearly demonstrated that some companies are **vulnerable** to takeovers."
— T. Boone Pickens, Jr., Chairman, Mesa Petroleum, in *Planning Review*

Accountants might be considered **invulnerable** to recessions because someone must keep track of the red ink.

- QUIZ -

Match the Tier II word in the first column with its synonym in the second column.

_____	1. unprecedented	a.	set right
_____	2. validate	b.	clear
_____	3. vindicate	c.	break
_____	4. unequivocal	d.	change one's mind
_____	5. vociferous	e.	new
_____	6. versatile	f.	unstable
_____	7. usurp	g.	workable
_____	8. violate	h.	grab
_____	9. vacillate	i.	unproven
_____	10. volatile	j.	confirm
_____	11. viable	k.	weak
_____	12. unsubstantiated	l.	generally capable
_____	13. vulnerable	m.	loud
_____	14. unilateral	n.	instinctive
_____	15. vicarious	o.	felt through other
_____	16. visceral	p.	not mutual

Answers:

1. e	5. m	9. d	13. k
2. j	6. l	10. f	14. p
3. a	7. h	11. g	15. o
4. b	8. c	12. i	16. n

Review Letters T-U-V

Choose the word from this section that most closely approximates the italicized words in the sentences below.

PART A

1. Please *send* this message by fax. t_____

2. The former dictator planned to *seize* power through a coup. u_____

3. Rose won't *put up with* messy handwriting. t_____

4. Our department, which is overstaffed, felt especially *defenseless* when we heard the news about layoffs. v_____

5. We must present a *defensible* plan to the board of directors. t_____

6. I had an *instinctive* sense that something bad was about to happen. (a) v_____

7. Todd tends to irritate everyone by making *incidental* observations during serious discussions. t_____

8. Both parties felt it was a successful *business deal*. t_____

9. The book about jet fighters let me experience the adventure *through others*. v_____

PART B

1. Given this *changeable* market, I would not ask for a raise. v_____

2. Grace was *insistent* about going ahead with the new project. v_____

3. Shifting priorities caused *great confusion* in the steel industry. t_____

4. I trust you will not *break* our agreement. v_____

5. Every year the motor vehicles department must *formally approve* your right to drive. v_____

6. Even a small mathematical error could *stain* your reputation as a genius. t_____

7. The highway will *end* just outside the city. t_____

8. The former enemies held an *unheard-of* summit meeting. u_____

9. The negotiators opposed any action that was *not mutual*. u_____

PART C

1. I hope the new business venture will be commercially *workable*. v_____

2. The decade was a time of confusion and *change* in many parts of the world. t_____

3. The policeman's charges remain *unproven*. u_____

4. An investigation will *clear* me of any wrongdoing. v_____

5. Her ideas *go beyond* her experience. t_____

6. The congressman's defense of himself was *unqualified*. u_____

7. The manager's warning was *nearly* a threat. t_____ (to)

8. Robert's grasp of the material is *weak*. t_____

9. Noah can't be trusted over the long haul because he *changes his mind* about everything. v_____

10. The company was seeking someone with *broad capability* in media for the public relations job. (a) v_____

Answers

A. 1. transmit   4. vulnerable   7. tangential
2. usurp   5. tenable   8. transaction
3. tolerate   6. visceral   9. vicariously

B. 1. volatile   4. violate   7. terminate
2. vociferous   5. validate   8. unprecedented
3. turmoil   6. tarnish   9. unilateral

C. 1. viable   5. transcend   9. vacillates
2. transition   6. unequivocal   10. versatility
3. unsubstantiated   7. tantamount (to)
4. vindicate   8. tenuous

VIII Writer's Reference Guide

Whether you write for a profession, write memos and letters on the job or are a student, it will be helpful to have a guide to higher level words at your finger tips. The following handy writer's reference guide will enable you to more easily find the Tier II words in this book for which you are looking. Unlike a Thesaurus, which does not differentiate between Tier I, Tier II and Tier III words, this reference guide is arranged in alphabetical order of the Tier I words with the Tier II words indicated next to them. Please note that some of these Tier I and Tier II words are not exact synonyms but can be used interchangeably. Refer to Chapter VII for a more complete clarification of the Tier II words.

A

abnormal — *anomalous*

about to occur — *imminent*

abstract — *intangible*

accept — *acknowledge*

accidental — *inadvertent*

accurate — *meticulous*

acquire — *obtain*

actual — *substantive*

add to — *augment*

admit — *acknowledge*

agree with — *acquiesce*

agreeable — *conciliatory, congenial*

allow — *authorize*

alteration — *conversion*

amend — *revise*

anger — *antagonize*

angered — *infuriated*

answer — *respond*

anxious — *apprehensive*

appeal to — *implore*

appear — *manifest*

appoint — *designate*

approach — *address*

approve — *endorse, sanction*

(formally) approve — *validate*

argumentative — *contentious*

arouse — *galvanize, instigate*

arrogant — *presumptuous*
artistic — *aesthetic*
ask for — *solicit*
aspect — *dimension*
assert — *affirm*
assumed — *hypothetical*
assumption — *premise*
attraction — *affinity*
attractive — *aesthetic*
audacious — *presumptuous*
authority — *mandate*
authorize — *sanction*
aware — *cognizant*

B

bad — *deleterious*
(evoke) bad feeling — *antagonize*
(obviously) bad — *flagrant*
badmouth — *disparage*
baffle — *perplex*
balance — *equilibrium*
barrier — *impediment*
base — *predicate*
basic — *fundamental*
bear — *tolerate*
bearing — *demeanor*
beat to the punch (colloq.) — *preempt*
(dealing with the) beautiful — *aesthetic*
beg — *implore*
begin — *initiate*
beginning (adj.)— *embryonic*
beginning (n.)— *inception*

belief — *conviction*
(hard to) believe — *implausible*
belittle — *denigrate, disparage*
belligerent — *contentious*
bent — *affinity*
bequest — *legacy*
(make) better — *ameliorate*
(go) beyond — *transcend*
blacken — *tarnish*
blame — *culpability*
blameworthy — *reprehensible*
blend (n.)— *synthesis*
blend (v.)— *integrate*
bliss — *euphoria*
(stumbling) block — *impediment*
bother — *chagrin*
(able to) bounce back — *resilient*
boundary — *parameter*
brainwash — *indoctrinate*
brand negatively — *stigmatize*
breach — *violate*
break — *violate*
break down — *malfunction*
breakdown — *debacle*
breaking (of rules) — *infraction*
bring about — *precipitate*
bring back — *restore*
bring to light — *elicit*
bully — *intimidate*
buoyant — *resilient*
burdensome — *onerous*
business agreement — *transaction*
bypass — *circumvent*

C

call for — *advocate*

cancel out — *neutralize*

(generally) capable — *versatile*

careful — *prudent*

(very) careful — *meticulous*

carry out — *execute, implement*

cast off — *repudiate*

cause — *precipitate*

cease — *expire*

censure — *reprimand*

certain — *infallible*

(act of making more) certain — *corroboration*

change (n.) — *conversion, transition*

change (v.) — *fluctuate, revise*

change back — *revert*

change mind — *vacillate*

changeable — *capricious, volatile*

changeover — *conversion*

chaos — *turmoil*

characteristic — *attribute*

charge — *allege*

cheerful — *sanguine*

chew away — *erode*

(difficult) choice — *dilemma*

(unsatisfactory) choice — *dilemma*

choose — *elect*

claim — *allege*

clear (adj.) — *explicit, unequivocal*

clear (v.) — *vindicate*

close at hand — *imminent*

collapse — *debacle*

collect — *compile*

combative — *belligerent*

combination — *synthesis*

combine — *integrate*

combined action — *synergy*

come between — *intervene*

command — *mandate*

common — *prevalent, generic*

comparable — *analogous (to)*

competition — *rivalry*

complete — *comprehensive*

compose — *constitute*

conceal — *suppress*

concern oneself with — *address*

conclude — *terminate*

conclusion from appearances — *conjecture*

conclusive — *definitive*

condemnable — *deplorable, reprehensible*

confirm — *substantiate, validate*

confirmation — *corroboration*

(act of) confirming — *corroboration*

confuse — *perplex*

confused — *ambivalent*

confusing — *obscure*

confusion — *disarray*

(great) confusion — *turmoil*

connected — *coherent*

conscious — *cognizant*

consequence — *ramification*

consider — *contemplate*

consistent — *coherent*

(overly) content — *complacent*
contradictory — *paradox*
contrast — *differentiate*
control — *manipulate*
conversation — *dialogue*
convey — *transmit*
cooperate — *collaborate*
cooperative action — *synergy*
correct — *rectify, revise*
covert — *surreptitious*
crazy — *bizarre*
crazy about — *enamored*
criticize — *reprimand*
crude — *visceral*
current — *prevalent*
cursory — *superficial*
customary — *prevalent*
cutback — *curtailment*

D

damaging — *detrimental*
danger — *jeopardize*
dangerous — *precarious*
deal — *transaction*
death — *demise*
debate — *controversy*
decide — *elect*
decisive — *definitive*
declare — *affirm, allege*
decline — *atrophy, deteriorate*
decreasing in size or number — *attrition*
deeply felt — *profound*
defenseless — *vulnerable*
defensible — *tenable*

definite — *explicit, unequivocal*
definition — *delineation*
demonstrate — *illustrate*
deny — *refute*
deportment — *demeanor*
derogatory reference — *innuendo*
description — *delineation*
desire — *aspiration*
destroy — *erode, invalidate*
detail — *enumerate*
detect — *discern*
determine — *ascertain*
develop — *evolve*
developing — *embryonic*
deviation — *aberration*
devise — *formulate*
devoted to others — *altruistic*
dictatorial — *arbitrary*
die — *perish*
difference — *disparity*
difference of opinion — *controversy*
(make) different — *differentiate*
difficult — *formidable, onerous*
difficult to solve — *problematical*
difficulty — *adversity*
dirty — *tarnish*
disagreement — *controversy*
disaster — *debacle*
disbelieving — *incredulous*
disclaim — *repudiate*
(creating) discord — *divisiveness*
discourage — *dissuade*
discover — *ascertain*

discrepancy — *incongruity*

discretionary — *arbitrary*

discussion — *dialogue*

disengage — *extricate*

disgrace — *humiliation*

disgraceful — *reprehensible*

dishonor — *tarnish*

disillusionment — *disenchantment*

dismay — *chagrin*

disorder — *disarray, turmoil*

disown — *repudiate*

disprove — *invalidate, refute*

(creating) dissension — *divisiveness*

distinguish — *differentiate*

distinguished — *preeminent*

distress — *adversity, chagrin*

distribute — *disseminate*

do — *execute*

do well — *flourish*

double bind — *dilemma*

doubtful — *implausible, problematical, skeptical*

doubting — *incredulous*

down-to-earth (colloq.) — *pragmatic, mundane*

draw out — *elicit*

dubious — *implausible*

dull remark — *platitude*

dying — *demise*

E

(too) early — *premature*

effect — *ramification*

effect (often remote, indirect) — *repercussions*

elastic — *resilient*

elation — *euphoria*

element — *dimension*

(insincere) eloquence — *rhetoric*

embarrassment — *humiliation*

emotion — *sentiment*

end (n.)— *demise*

end (v.)— *expire, terminate*

endanger — *imperil*

endangered — *jeopardize*

energetic — *dynamic*

enlarge — *augment*

enormous — *prodigious*

enraged — *infuriated*

entitle — *authorize*

equal — *tantamount*

(try to) equal — *emulate*

equivalent — *tantamount*

essential — *indispensable*

estrange — *alienate*

evade — *circumvent, equivocate*

event — *phenomenon*

evoke — *elicit*

examine — *scrutinize*

example — *paradigm*

exceed — *transcend*

excessive — *inordinate, intolerable*

excite — *galvanize*

exclusive — *proprietary*

excuse — *condone, vindicate*
execute — *implement*
expect — *anticipate*
expire — *perish*
explosive — *volatile*
exposed — *vulnerable*
express clearly — *articulate*
extensive — *pervasive*
extent — *magnitude, spectrum*
eyeball — *scrutinize*

F

faith — *conviction*
false — *fictitious*
false belief — *illusion*
fantastic — *bizarre*
fantasy — *illusion*
favorable — *auspicious*
fearful — *apprehensive*
fearfully concerned —
    apprehensive
feasible — *viable*
feeling — *intuition, sentiment*
felt through others — *vicarious*
final — *definitive, irrevocable*
find out — *ascertain*
firm — *resolute*
fix (n.) — *dilemma*
fix (v.) — *rectify*
fixed — *resolute*
flexible — *resilient*
flimsy — *tenuous*
follow — *adhere*
foolproof — *infallible*
force — *compel*

forceful — *dynamic, emphatic*
forerunner — *harbinger*
foresee — *anticipate*
forfeit — *sacrifice*
forgive — *condone*
form — *constitute*
formless — *amorphous*
found — *predicate*
frank — *candid*
friendly — *conciliatory,
    congenial*
frighten — *intimidate*
fulfill — *implement*
fusion — *synthesis*

G

gain — *attain*
gain an advantage — *preempt*
gather — *compile*
general — *generic*
get — *obtain*
get back — *retaliate*
get even — *retaliate*
get off topic— *digress*
get out of — *extricate*
get worse — *deteriorate*
gift — *legacy*
give back — *restore*
give in — *acquiesce, capitulate*
give life to — *animate*
give up — *capitulate,
    relinquish, sacrifice*
giving — *benevolent*
glaring — *flagrant*
gloomy — *ominous*

go around — *circumvent*
goal — *aspiration*
good — *beneficial, benevolent*
good judgment — *discretion*
grab — *usurp*
graceful — *aesthetic*
group — *aggregate, coalition*
grow — *evolve*
grow quickly — *proliferate*
guess — *conjecture, speculate*
guideline — *parameter*
guilt — *culpability*

H

handle — *manipulate*
happening — *phenomenon*
hard-to-get — *elusive*
hard to pin down — *elusive*
harm — *impair*
harmful — *deleterious, detrimental, inimical*
harmless — *innocuous*
hassle — *turmoil*
have to do with — *pertain (to)*
heighten — *enhance, intensify*
heritage — *legacy*
hesitate — *vacillate*
hide — *suppress*
hint — *innuendo*
hold — *retain*
hold back — *refrain*
honest — *candid*
hope — *aspiration*
hopeful — *sanguine*
hostile — *adversarial, inimical*

(make) hostile — *alienate*
(evoke) hostility — *antagonize*
huge — *prodigious*
hunch — *intuition*
hurt — *impair*

I

ideal — *paradigm*
(nearly) identical — *tantamount*
ignorance — *provincialism*
(evoke) ill will — *antagonize*
imaginary — *fictitious*
imagine — *envision, speculate*
imitate with a view to outdo — *emulate*
important — *substantive*
improve — *ameliorate, enhance*
inappropriateness — *incongruity*
inattentive — *inadvertent*
incapable of error — *infallible*
incidental — *tangential*
inclination — *propensity*
(all) inclusive — *comprehensive*
inconsistency — *incongruity*
inconsistent — *paradox*
incorrect — *erroneous*
increase — *augment, enhance, intensify*
incredible — *inconceivable*
indecisive — *vacillate*
indefinite — *problematical*
indifferent — *apathetic*
inequality — *disparity*
(assign to) inferior position — *relegate*

inflexible — *intransigent*
influence — *manipulate*
innately — *inherently*
(substitution of) inoffensive
    word for more unpleasant
    one — *euphemism*
insignificant — *inconsequential*
insistent — *emphatic, vociferous*
inspect — *scrutinize*
instinctive — *visceral*
instruct — *indoctrinate*
interfere — *intervene*
interval — *interim*
invite — *solicit*
involvement — *intervene*
irregular — *anomalous,
    intermittent*

J

join forces — *collaborate*
joy — *euphoria*

K

keep — *retain*
keep from doing something —
    refrain
keep up — *perpetuate*
kind — *benevolent*
(make) known — *divulge*

L

label negatively — *stigmatize*
(high-flown) language — *rhetoric*
leave out — *omit*

lessen — *alleviate, diminish,
    mitigate*
let go (of) — *relinquish*
like — *analogous (to)*
limit — *parameter*
list — *enumerate*
(make) lively — *animate*
logical — *coherent*
look at carefully — *scrutinize*
(on) looking back — *retrospect*
(a) lot — *abundance*
loud — *vociferous*
(in) love with — *enamored*
lower — *diminish*

M

made up — *fictitious*
maintain — *sustain*
maintainable — *tenable*
make — *compel*
make something last —
    perpetuate
make easier — *facilitate*
make up (for) — *compensate*
make up — *constitute*
making up — *reconciliation*
mark negatively — *stigmatize*
mass — *aggregate*
meantime — *interim*
measure — *criterion*
mechanical — *perfunctory*
mediate — *intervene*
meet — *comply (with)*
merciless — *relentless*
mess — *disarray*

misfortune — *adversity*

misinterpret — *misconstrue*

misread — *misconstrue*

mistaken — *erroneous*

mistrustful — *skeptical*

misunderstood — *misconstrue*

mixed — *ambivalent*

model — *paradigm*

moderate — *mitigate*

motivation — *impetus*

(period of) movement — *transition*

multiply — *proliferate*

(not) mutual — *unilateral*

mysterious — *inscrutable*

N

narrowness of mind — *provincialism*

native — *indigenous, intrinsic*

natural — *indigenous, intrinsic*

natural instinct — *intuition*

naturally — *inherently*

near — *imminent*

necessary — *indispensable*

necessity — *imperative*

negate — *invalidate*

negative — *deleterious*

negligent — *inadvertent*

new — *unprecedented*

noisy — *vociferous*

not easily lead — *intractable*

not well known — *obscure*

notice — *discern, perceive*

(take) notice of — *acknowledge*

novel — *unprecedented*

nullify — *invalidate*

O

obey — *comply (with)*

obligatory for — *incumbent on*

obliging — *conciliatory*

obsolete — *antiquated*

obstacle — *impediment*

obvious — *overt*

occurrence — *phenomenon*

of two minds — *ambivalent*

offer up — *sacrifice*

offset — *neutralize*

okay — *endorse*

old — *antiquated*

omen — *harbinger*

on-and-off — *intermittent*

(relating to) one side only — *unilateral*

one who thinks people are motivated only by self-interest — *cynic*

onset — *inception*

open — *candid, overt*

open (to attack) — *vulnerable*

opinion — *conviction, sentiment*

opposing — *adversarial*

opposite of what is expected — *irony*

opposition — *rivalry*

oppressive — *onerous*

optimistic — *sanguine*

order — *mandate*

(place in lower) order — *subordinate*

ordinary — *mundane*
out-of-date — *antiquated*
out of place — *anomalous*
outer — *external*
outline — *delineation*
outmoded — *antiquated*
outrageous — *flagrant*
outside — *external*
outward — *external*
outward manner — *demeanor*
overcome — *prevail*
overlook — *condone*
overstepping bounds — *presumptuous*

P

pacify — *appease*
pardon — *condone*
patching up — *reconciliation*
pay — *compensate*
pay back — *compensate, reciprocate, retaliate*
(well) paying — *lucrative*
peace-making — *conciliatory*
peerless — *preeminent*
perform — *execute*
performed in place of another — *vicarious*
periodic — *intermittent*
peripheral — *tangential*
permit — *authorize, sanction*
person who holds an office — *incumbent*
petty — *inconsequential, superficial*
picture — *envision*

pipe dream — *illusion*
pitiful — *deplorable*
plan — *formulate*
plead with — *implore*
pleasant — *congenial*
plenty — *abundance*
point of view — *perspective*
point out — *designate*
poor — *impoverish*
poverty — *impoverish*
powerful — *formidable, invincible*
practical — *pragmatic*
precise — *meticulous*
prepare for — *anticipate*
preserve — *perpetuate*
prevent — *preclude*
privately owned — *proprietary*
privilege — *prerogative*
(difficult) problem — *dilemma*
profitable — *lucrative*
promising — *auspicious*
prove — *substantiate*
provoke — *antagonize, instigate, precipitate*
prudence— *discretion*
public — *overt*
put down — *denigrate, disparage*
put together — *compile, formulate, integrate*
put up with — *tolerate*
puzzle — *perplex*
puzzling — *paradox*

Q

(relating to) qualities — *qualitative*

quality — *attribute*

quarrelsome — *belligerent, contentious*

question — *issue*

quicken — *accelerate*

R

ramble — *digress*

random — *arbitrary*

range — *spectrum*

(place in lower) rank — *subordinate*

reach — *attain*

react — *respond*

real — *intrinsic, substantive*

realistic — *pragmatic*

rebuke — *reprimand*

(tending to) recall — *reminiscent*

recommend — *advocate*

reduce — *diminish, mitigate, subordinate*

reduction — *curtailment*

refer (to) — *pertain (to)*

refill — *replenish*

(on) reflection — *retrospect*

regress — *revert*

regret — *contrition*

reject — *repudiate*

relate (to) — *pertain (to)*

release — *extricate*

relieve — *alleviate*

(relating to) remembered experience — *reminiscent*

(tending to) remind — *reminiscent*

remorse — *contrition*

repay — *compensate*

repeat — *reiterate*

replace — *supersede*

reply — *respond*

request — *solicit*

require — *compel*

required of — *incumbent on*

requirement — *imperative*

(state of being) reserved — *reticence*

respond in kind — *reciprocate*

restate — *reiterate*

restock — *replenish*

restrained — *reticence*

result — *ramification*

resupply — *replenish*

return — *restore, revert*

return the favor — *reciprocate*

reveal — *divulge*

reveal (itself) — *manifest*

rewarding — *beneficial*

ridicule — *irony*

right — *prerogative*

risk — *imperil, jeopardize*

risky — *precarious*

(well) rounded — *versatile*

rout — *debacle*

routine — *mundane*

run out (colloq.) — *expire*

S

sad — *deplorable*

(light) sarcasm — *irony*

satisfy — *appease, comply (with)*

save — *retain*

say — *affirm, articulate*

scare — *intimidate*

scatter — *dissipate*

schism — *dichotomy*

(on) second thought — *retrospect*

secret — *surreptitious*

(keep) secret — *suppress*

(very) secure — *invincible*

see — *discern, envision, perceive*

seize upon — *preempt*

seize wrongfully — *usurp*

select — *designate*

self-satisfied — *complacent*

send — *transmit*

sense — *intuition*

sensible — *prudent*

set apart — *designate*

set in motion — *activate*

set off — *differentiate*

set right — *rectify, vindicate*

settlement — *reconciliation*

shallow — *superficial*

shame — *humiliation*

shameful — *deplorable, reprehensible*

shapeless — *amorphous*

sharp division — *dichotomy*

sharpen — *intensify*

shift — *transition*

shifty — *elusive*

short-lived — *ephemeral*

shortening — *curtailment*

show — *illustrate*

show (itself) — *manifest*

shrink — *diminish*

sign — *harbinger*

similar — *analogous (to)*

simplify — *facilitate*

size — *dimension, magnitude*

skeptical — *incredulous*

skip — *omit*

slight — *nominal*

slippery — *elusive*

small — *inconsequential, nominal*

smug — *complacent*

sneaky — *surreptitious*

(too) soon — *premature*

soothe — *appease*

sorrow — *contrition*

speak to — *address*

specific — *explicit*

specify — *enumerate*

speed up — *accelerate*

split — *dichotomy*

spread — *dissipate*

spread quickly — *proliferate*

spread widely — *disseminate*

stain — *tarnish*

stand — *tolerate*

standard — *criterion*

start (n.) — *inception*

start (v.) — *activate, initiate, instigate*

state — *affirm*

state without proof — *allege*

steadfast — *resolute*

step in — *intervene*

stick to — *adhere to*

stimulate — *galvanize*

stimulus — *impetus*

stop — *terminate*

straightforward — *candid*

strange — *bizarre*

strengthen — *intensify*

strict — *relentless*

stubborn — *intractable, intransigent*

study — *contemplate*

subject — *issue*

subjective — *arbitrary*

subtle — *intangible*

succeed — *flourish, prevail*

suggestion — *innuendo*

suggestive — *reminiscent*

superficial — *perfunctory*

superior — *preeminent*

supplant — *supersede*

support — *adhere, advocate, endorse, sustain*

supportable — *tenable*

supposed — *hypothetical*

surface — *superficial*

surpass — *transcend*

surrender — *capitulate*

suspicion — *conjecture*

suspicious — *skeptical*

switch — *conversion*

sympathetic understanding — *empathy*

(relating to) system — *systemic*

T

tact — *discretion*

take — *usurp*

take the place of — *preempt*

talk — *dialogue*

talk to — *address*

teach uncritically — *indoctrinate*

tell — *divulge*

tendency — *propensity*

test — *criterion*

(list of) things to be done — *agenda*

think deeply about — *contemplate*

thinning out — *attrition*

thorough — *comprehensive*

(not) thorough — *superficial*

threatening — *ominous*

thrive — *flourish*

timely — *auspicious*

topic — *issue*

(list of) topics — *agenda*

total — *aggregate*

tough — *formidable*

(relating to) traits — *qualitative*

transfer — *relegate*

transient — *ephemeral*

tremendous — *prodigious*

trigger — *instigate, precipitate*

trite remark — *platitude*

triumph — *prevail*

trouble — *adversity*
turn against — *alienate*
turn aside — *dissuade*
turn back — *revert*
turn off — *alienate*
turn on — *activate*
two opposing factions or views
    — *polarize*

U

unbearable — *intolerable*
unbelievable — *inconceivable*
unbelieving — *incredulous*
unbending — *intransigent,
    relentless*
uncertain — *problematical*
unchangeable — *irrevocable*
unclear — *ambiguous, obscure*
uncommunicative — *reticence*
unconcerned — *apathetic*
unconfirmed — *unsubstantiated*
unconquerable — *invincible*
uncontrollable — *intractable*
undefinable — *intangible*
underlying — *fundamental*
understood — *implicit*
undeveloped — *embryonic*
unequal — *disproportionate*
unerring — *infallible*
uneven — *disproportionate*
unfair — *inequitable*
unfavorable — *inimical*
(highly) unfavorable — *ominous*
unfeeling — *perfunctory*
unhappiness — *disenchantment*

unheard-of — *unprecedented*
unimportant — *inconsequential*
uninterested — *apathetic*
unite — *integrate*
unjust — *inequitable*
unknowable — *inscrutable*
unknown — *obscure*
unlikely — *implausible*
unmanageable — *intractable*
unproven — *unsubstantiated*
unqualified — *unequivocal*
unreasonable — *arbitrary,
    inordinate*
unrelated — *tangential*
unsafe — *precarious*
unselfish — *altruistic*
unsettled — *problematical*
unspoken — *implicit*
unstable — *capricious, volatile*
unsuitability — *incongruity*
unusual — *aberration,
    anomalous*
unusually large —
    disproportionate
unverified — *unsubstantiated*
unyielding — *intransigent*
urge — *advocate*
useful — *beneficial*

V

vague — *ambiguous, amorphous*
vague — *intangible*
vary — *fluctuate*
verbal exchange — *dialogue*
verify — *substantiate*

very bad — *deplorable*

view (n.) — *conviction, perspective*

view (v.)— *perceive*

viewpoint — *perspective*

violation — *infraction*

vital — *indispensable*

W

waffle — *equivocate*

wander — *digress*

warlike — *belligerent*

waste — *dissipate*

waste away — *atrophy*

waver — *vacillate*

weak — *tenuous, vulnerable*

weaken — *debilitate, impair*

wear away — *erode*

(gradual) wearing down — *attrition*

whimsical — *arbitrary, capricious*

widespread — *pervasive, prevalent*

win — *prevail*

wise — *prudent*

wondrous — *prodigious*

work improperly — *malfunction*

work together — *collaborate*

workable — *viable*

worried — *apprehensive*

worsen — *deteriorate, exacerbate*

wrong — *erroneous*

Y

yield — *relinquish*

IX A Final Note

If you have completed this book, you've learned that the secret to an excellent spoken vocabulary is surprisingly simple. Substitute more Tier II words—words that you comprehend and perhaps use on occasion—for the simple Tier I words that you generally use in ordinary conversation.

Keep in mind that the vocabulary words included in this book represent a broad spectrum of the words used by leaders—but are not an all-inclusive list. And even the most successful leaders use simple words. It is neither possible nor desirable to exclude simple words from our word bank. Ideally, you can achieve an appropriate balance by increasing the proportion of higher level words in your daily conversation.

If you have studied this book and have been diligent in your efforts to substitute Tier II words for Tier I words, you've taken an important step toward enhancing and furthering your career. To be successful, however, it is imperative that you incorporate these valuable words into your daily vocabulary. If you do so, you will have achieved your goal: You will speak with a balanced and enriched vocabulary that will make you more interesting, authoritative, and professional. And you will be expressing yourself with the words leaders use—a vocabulary for success.

Bibliography

Lincoln Barnett, *The Treasure of Our Tongue*, Alfred A. Knopf, 1964.

Hugh Kenner, Ph.D, "Neatness Doesn't Count After All," *Discover*, April 1986.

Mario Pei, *The Story of Language*, Mentor Books, 1965.

Richard M. Smith, Ph.D., Gary P. Supanish, "The Vocabulary Scores of Company Presidents," Johnson O'Connor Research Foundation, Human Engineering Laboratory, 1984.

"Voices/Should the USA build more nuclear power plants?" *USA Today*, March 11, 1991.

"Reviving Nuclear Power From Its Coma," *The New York Times*, November 18, 1990.

Notes

Notes

Notes

Notes

DASHIR Mail Sales
458 Reis Ave.
Teaneck, NJ 07666

Please send me _____ copy(ies) of *WORD POWER: Vocabulary for Success.*

I am enclosing $7.95 per book ($8.95 in Canada) + $2.95 for handling and postage for the first book and $1 for each additional book for a total of $_____. (Please include appropriate state sales tax.) Send check or money order — no cash or C.O.D's please. Valid in US and Canada only. All orders are subject to availability of books.

_____

Name

_____

Address

_____

City   *State*   *Zip*

Allow at least 4–6 weeks for delivery.

Phone Orders

Call 1–800–356–9315 to order by credit card. Allow 2–3 weeks for delivery.

About the Author

Charles Ickowicz (ī-kō-witz) is a Market Development Manager with a major international chemical company. His background includes consulting and strategic planning.

Raised in Omaha, Nebraska, he earned a BS in Chemistry from Creighton University in Omaha and an MBA from New York University in New York City.

Mr. Ickowicz resides in Teaneck, New Jersey with his wife, Helen, and two children, Shira and David.

WORD POWER: Vocabulary for Success, his first book, is a result of his fascination with the historical development of vocabulary and language.